FROM FATHERLESS TO
FATHERHOOD

OMAR EPPS

ISBN: 978-1-4834-8503-4 (sc)
ISBN: 978-1-4834-8504-1 (hc)
ISBN: 978-1-4834-8505-8 (e)

Library of Congress Control Number: 2018905170

Lulu Publishing Services rev. date: 5/31/2018

No doubt about it: children are a gift from the LORD;
the fruit of the womb is a divine reward.
—Psalm 123:3 (American Standard Version)

Contents

Introduction

"I'm here, ain't I?"

That's the thought I had one day after having worked for fifteen hours. As soon as I arrived home, my wife asked me to spend some time with our son, and for some reason I was slightly bothered by the tone of her question. As I flopped onto the couch, turned on CNN, and took off my shoes to rub my aching feet, I thought, *What more do you want? Isn't this the life that I promised?* I've been in the entertainment business for more than twenty-five years, and since my very first film, I've fought tooth and nail for respect. And that fight continues. Nothing is guaranteed in this business, so when it comes to my family, I make sure they reap all the benefits. I continuously sacrifice myself for our betterment. So who could question me in that regard?

"I'm here, ain't I?"

Moments after having that thought, I realized how selfish it was. But more importantly, I became very interested in the origins of such a thought. My son doesn't care if he rides shotgun in a Range Rover, wears nice clothes, or plays every game that Xbox offers. It's not my children's fault they're accustomed to a life I didn't have growing up. I realized that my father's absence in my own childhood may have somehow crept into my full understanding of the responsibilities and sacrifices of fatherhood, and with this realization, the seeds to write this book were planted.

Since my biological father had been completely absent from my life, I thought my presence was a present to my family. I was dead wrong.

Before getting up from the couch, I tried to rationalize what I'd felt, but all I came up with were excuses. I owed my wife an apology, but first, I needed to check on my son. I was hungry, exhausted, and agitated, but that comes with the territory of being a parent. Parents put their children first. And I don't get a pass because I'm Omar Epps. Just like I was as a child, my son is the only boy in our immediate family, and it's my responsibility to provide him with that daily dose of fatherly love, even when I'm tired and want to relax. As I walked to my son's room, I felt like I was walking through a different chamber of consciousness. As I got closer, I heard him playing and making roller-coaster sounds. Before I walked in, I smiled proudly as I peeked inside of his room. When I think back to this moment, I feel obligated to dig deeper into myself, and the history of my own childhood. I feel driven to dive headfirst into the depths of the torment and the pain I've felt toward my father for the lack of his presence in my life. Welcome to my story …

CHAPTER 1

From Whence I Came

It's not the presents, it's your presence and the essence of being there and showing the baby that you care.
—Ed O.G. & Da Bulldogs, "Be a Father to Your Child"

The place is Brooklyn, New York. Where dreams can become reality or a figment of the imagination. Brooklyn is a place where generations of immigrants came for decades from various countries seeking a better life for themselves and their families. It's one of the major cities in the United States where independent, free blacks settled by the thousands searching for a safe haven in the 1830s. It has spawned many successful entrepreneurs, politicians, entertainers, and athletes, as well as a plethora of infamous, notorious gangsters and such. Brooklyn, New York, is where I was born and raised.

My mother, Bonnie Epps-Burgess, was and still is my rock and pillar. She too was born in Brooklyn, the oldest of her five siblings. And she was ingrained with the will to not only survive, but to thrive in her existence. My parents dated for a couple of years and were married when I was born, but they divorced when I was two years old. To have my mom tell it, the next six years of my life involving my father were filled with many sporadic disappointments, hopes that were raised and shattered, and expectations that were lifted only to be let down. The only constant I can recall from those times is my father's deafening absence. What kept me content was the abundance of love I received from my mother. She truly is a superwoman. I watched her rise through the ranks of the New York City Board of Education—from a teacher, to an assistant principal, to a principal, to the deputy superintendent of twenty-six schools in New York City's public school system. I have no clue how she found the time or energy to also volunteer on various committees and involve herself deeply with her sorority, Delta Sigma Theta Sorority Inc. My mom sought to provide me with all the comforts any young boy would want. And at an early age, she exposed me to the arts, sports, and summer camp up in Pennsylvania. Although we didn't have a lot of money, I never felt as though we were poor. My childhood was rich with love and laughter!

A few years after the riots of 1968, the subsequent destruction of the Black Panther Party, and James Brown's groundbreaking song "Say It Loud," it seemed as though the activists—and fathers—within the black community began to either die out or face life in prison. The dynamics of the black family structure were in disarray. "Power to the people" was the mantra, and a black fist in the air was worth a thousand words. Five years later, I was born in the ghetto but destined to become a king. I was raised amid a surge of Afrocentricity, knowledge of self, and black unity, along with rampant crime, shootings, stabbings, and murders. All the while, just a hop, skip, and jump away from Wall Street, where the money movers of the world did their biddings. A societal shift seemed to be under way, and a lot of black men from the generation prior to mine became stagnant. They emulated the images of the pimps and drug dealers who were glorified in blaxploitation films. We knew the portrayals of our people in those films were mostly negative. Still, a skewed perception of our culture hit big screens. Pimp takes over the city while threatening to smack his prostitutes if they fail to make his quota. Pimp preys on young, downtrodden women, all for the love of money. Manipulates their minds just to turn their temples into a cheap alley thrill for a buck.

Nothing about those messages and images improved the black family structure. And even after James Brown's attempt to restore black pride through song, black people continued to flock to the theaters to see blaxploitation films. Now of course, some of those early films gave us our first glimpses of black action heroes, like Shaft and such. But those films were made before the term *blaxploitation* had even been coined. Certain films of the time, like the iconic *Sweet Sweetback's Baadasssss Song*, were thought-provoking, progressive works of art. I'm not referring to those types of films when I'm speaking about blaxploitation on-screen. I'm talking about those B&D kind of films that glorified pimps, hustlers, and prostitutes. Though it's common to hear a prostitute call her pimp "Daddy," everything about a pimp is the exact opposite of a true father. A pimp is selfish and unloving, and he will discard a human life as if it were a piece of trash. Needless to say, a generation of so-called pimps were born, and images of positive black fatherhood would take a back seat. We'd accepted a fictional, fetishized depiction of our culture, and our communities paid a hefty price.

The era of blaxploitation was sputtering to an end when a beacon of light called *Good Times* broke through for the better. The purpose of *Good Times* was to explore the dynamics of a struggling black family living in the projects. It was through this TV show that I first saw a living example of an active black father. With the rest of the country, I hummed along to the catchy theme song, and every afternoon I got a glimpse of what it would be like to have a father in the household. The lead male character, James Evans, was a loving individual with integrity and, sometimes, foolish pride. He understood the social imbalances and even risked his life to provide for his family. He despised the ways of the pimps and drug dealers. And he restored an image of fatherhood that was honorable in the eyes of the underprivileged. The Evans family grew up in conditions that were similar to those of every child in the projects, but there was one major difference: their father was present.

Long before that show, my father had proved to me that he didn't possess the same principles of James Evans. He'd forfeited his responsibilities as my protector and provider and become the definition of a rolling stone. He was unsuccessful in exhibiting the courage it takes to rise above one's circumstances, at least when it came to me. And though my mom was a superwoman, of course she struggled as a single parent. As I grew older, I questioned why the men in my life weren't really present. Needless to say, I was left to figure things out on my own. Here and there my grandfather, rest his soul, would sit me down and give me lessons that only a grandfather could, but he never really took me under his wing in that regard. I'd see my uncle on holidays and such, but I guess he was busy figuring out his own issues as a young man. I was too young to be in tune with the generational pattern of fatherlessness within my own family. Therefore, at a very young age, I buried that disappointment deep in my heart and moved on the best way I could.

When I was around seven years old, my mother dated a Chinese American guy. Whenever people saw us together, I could feel their judgmental eyes trying to understand the dichotomy of our relationship. Fortunately for me, he didn't care what people thought, and his sentiment rubbed off on me. I appreciated how he openly expressed his love for me, but with me being so young, our connection only compounded a deep-rooted problem brewing within my spirit. Society indoctrinates us with a narrow, black-and-white perspective of what the normal social paradigm should be. Even though my relationship with him broadened my perspective, I'd often wonder, where was the man who looked like me? Where was my biological James Evans? With every episode of *Good Times*, I saw what love could look like between a father and son. So, in a sense, each episode reminded me that I didn't have that.

On the surface, he appeared to be your stereotypical Chinese American dude who maybe ran a Laundromat somewhere in Brooklyn. However, he was very different. He loved skiing and R&B music, and he had style. More importantly, he loved my mother. I still enjoyed watching *Good Times*, but my reality at the time was slightly different from what was being portrayed on the show. It depicted raw imagery and underlying messages of hope, but I knew that sense of hope wasn't all the way real. Nothing drove that point home more than when James Evans died. With the rest of the hood, I'd waited for the big break that would take the Evans family out of the projects and into the good life. But that never happened. In my opinion, such a message perpetuated the idea that success was never really around the corner for black people. And "keeping your head above water" was more than a lyric or idiom; it was a literal way of life for many of us.

I have fond memories of him taking me to the Vernon Valley Ski Resort. He was really the first man to show me the world was much bigger than my four-square-block radius. Asian or not, he was my first real definition of a father figure. He was the reason I fell in love with the sport of football. He was also the reason I played for the Brooklyn Skyhawks, a Pop Warner league team. But, even though he was present at my games, whenever I saw a black son with his biological father, I'd ponder very deeply on the inner workings of that relationship. While I was struggling to comprehend the mechanics of our own father-and-son bond, his relationship with my mother deteriorated. Soon after their breakup, I once again felt like most of the kids in the hood—fatherless, frustrated, and heartbroken. The void that he had unselfishly tried to fill was now open even wider. And though I had a constant abundance of love from my mother, at that time, I'd concluded that 50 percent of me was unknown.

Music has the power to communicate messages that words alone can't, and it can touch the body's chakras, creating a spiritual connection to sound. Some African traditions are imbued with the emotional and spiritual connection between music and humans. The Djembe drum, which dates back to AD 1000, was the underlying force within certain rituals and healing ceremonies, as well as being used to communicate with other tribes. Hip-hop music comes from this same deep-rooted vein. The power of music is beyond what we can see, and everyone can feel the energies that flow from the various forms of music. Rappers from the early '80s, like the Cold Crush Brothers and the Sugarhill Gang, were mostly into rocking parties with braggadocious raps and such. But those who came along later, like Public Enemy, coded their music with messages to uplift black culture. Hip-hop music taught me a lot about my African heritage and how our bloodlines from the motherland trace directly back to kings and queens. In 1986, hip-hop culture was coming into full effect, and pop-locking to a drum's heavy bass meant you had soul. Plus, back then some rappers used music as a tool to promote positivity and unity. At that time, my musical role models were speaking to me in a language I completely understood. For example, Grandmaster Flash and the Furious Five created a song called "White Lines" that was a warning about the perils associated with using cocaine. It spoke graphically about drug addiction and the subsequent destruction of those who succumb to drug addiction. It's amazing how hip-hop can influence the mind of a young child just in the confines of a three-minute song.

What if I'd given into the streets at that age and eventually been placed inside of a pine box because of the lack of my father's presence and guidance? Would he have even deserved the right to stand over my grave and weep? There's something terribly wrong with any parent who would leave his or her child's life up to chance.

As hip-hop culture continued to spread throughout the world, Mr. Magic's *Rap Attack* radio show and Ralph McDaniels's *Video Music Box* television show became staple outlets for the culture. If I wanted to know what to wear, the latest slang, and how to say it, all I had to do was tune in to those shows. Now, New York City is made up of five boroughs—Brooklyn, Queens, Manhattan, the Bronx, and Staten Island. Hip-hop started in the Bronx, but all New Yorkers know what it means when they hear "Is Brooklyn in the house?!" To understand the connection between hip-hop and urban communities, you have to look at it not only as a form of music but also as a complete lifestyle. Hip-hop culture was definitely persuasive to my young mind, with messages and imagery that would influence my development.

Unemployment was at an all-time high, war was on the horizon, and crack cocaine was sweeping through the black community like a tsunami. I was ten years old, and some days just playing outside was done at one's own risk. Simply put, the crack era was crazy! Crimes that were usually committed in the wee hours of the night turned into shootouts in broad day. Murder became normalized. When the neighborhood lights flickered on, mothers bellowed out their children's names from project windows. And if you were late getting home, a belt met your ass at the door. Young men were exterminating each other over fast money. I quickly went from being carefree to careful. In my mind, I was now of age to protect my mom from the madness in the streets.

During Ronald Reagan's presidency (also coined the Reaganomics era), inner-city men by the thousands were given extremely strict jail sentences. Back then politicians had no clue how to exert control and order over the newly minted drug lords in the impoverished communities, and their legislative approach further crippled the black family structure. They also made it difficult for ex-offenders to reestablish themselves in society after time served. While I don't condone criminal activity, a slew of those jail sentences simply didn't match up with the crimes committed. Some would argue it was a blatant attack, specifically against young black men. The Reaganomics era terrorized underprivileged urban families for decades, and fatherless children continued to fill up prison complexes. A lot of dudes became full-time criminals. Simultaneously, gangster rap became popular, providing the perfect soundtrack. Some of my peers began to live out the lyrics of rappers like Ice-T, and those dark messages created a kill-or-be-killed environment. Thus, the streets of Brooklyn became like the Wild, Wild West.

Without question an idle mind is easily fooled. So if kids don't have responsible parenting happening in their households, how can you blame them for emulating what they see being glorified in the streets? Whenever I watched *Video Music Box*, I wasn't just watching for the music videos; my mind was also yearning for the messages. Groups like Run-DMC would emerge, and the world was forced to adapt to the modern black experience.

Even though hip-hop culture gave me a sense of belonging, I was still just a kid. I vividly remember walking down the street and men whistling to get my mother's attention. Whenever I saw a man sizing my mother up in an unflattering, flirtatious manner, I was enraged. Some men would clutch their privates and utter disrespectful things to my mom, my queen and inspiration. It was as if to them, she was just another potential conquest. My mother always handled those situations with grace, but since I was still so young, I guess I felt vulnerable. In my mind, if someone ever touched her the wrong way, I would simply stab them to death. In reality, I was just a kid who probably couldn't stop a predator from snatching her away and doing the unthinkable. We'd walk through pockets of darkness to get home, and I would clench my fist and form the toughest face I could muster. Though things may seem okay on the surface, most times underneath a son's mean mug is a scared little boy.

My abilities in sports overshadowed my war within. I received accolades for playing football and was labeled a special player. The connection between star athletes and kids is unique. Of course I wanted to be like all the football greats, specifically Tony Dorsett, and I tried to emulate his athletic prowess on the football field. But I had no clue who he was, or how he acted off the field. Athletes' impact on how I developed as a boy was limited. The only connection I had to my favorite athletes was watching them play on television or having their player cards.

When I wasn't playing football, I was losing myself in my notebooks of poems and short stories. I vented on pieces of paper, and creatively I became sort of an introvert. The phrase "you'll see" was the fuel to my fire, and my father would be the first to feel the burn in my mind's eye. I never asked to be here—none of us did—but somehow I felt like the consequences of my parents' failed relationship had fallen into my lap. At a young age, I felt rage for my father's inability to foresee the impact of his absence in my life. My artistic expression helped me to navigate through that emotional maze. Nonetheless, I would've given anything to hear a meaningful explanation followed up with an apology from him. Something. Anything. Instead, he remained a mystery.

One day when I was twelve, my mom walked me to the store. To my surprise, she bought me a box of condoms. We'd had little talks here and there about sex, but I'd always shrugged it off. What preteen guy feels comfortable talking to his mom about sex, right? The main thing I knew was I'd better not get some girl pregnant. Still, her buying me my first box of condoms was completely out of the blue, and I wondered what brought about that sense of urgency for her. I wondered if she'd asked my uncle to speak to me about all that and he was too busy. Or did she assume my relationships with the men in the family weren't strong enough for a conversation of that magnitude? At twelve years old, I was robbed of experiencing "the man talk" with a man. Ironically, weeks after that awkward conversation with her, *Good Times* aired an episode dealing with the issues of sex.

I'm grateful she instinctively knew it was about that time, but a mother can't fully connect with her pubescent son in the same way a man can't fully connect with his daughter when she experiences her first menstrual cycle. Our roles to our children are essential. Most are shared, but others require the same gender. It's that simple. Historically, women have been forced into the masculine roles of raising boys into men the best way they can. The reasoning for such dates back to the 1600s, but how long can we blame the slave trade for current circumstances? We have to move forward. Slavery didn't stop my father from taking care of his fatherly responsibilities. He made a choice not to do so. Too many men of today have made a choice to leave the futures of their sons blowing in the wind.

Women share an unspoken, maternal responsibility to one another. As men, we should embrace the same. Men should feel obligated to engage in their fatherhood, not just spectate. Fatherhood in and of itself is the definition of true masculinity. For as long as I can remember, a lot of men have interpreted compassion as a form of weakness, and that incapacitates men to connect deeply to certain emotional frequencies. The ability to walk away from a child is a prime example of this disconnect. As we know, parenthood in general is circumstantial, but in general, mothers do not abandon their children. The majority of women feel an innate moral obligation to tend to their kids. So who gave men the right to ignore their moral obligations in that regard? When did fatherhood become just an option for men?

Okay, so the year was 1985, and it seemed like every two years my mom and I were moving to a new area in Brooklyn. As soon as I'd acclimated myself into a neighborhood and made friends, we'd move again. That rhythm gave me the ability to remove myself from personal connections quickly, which became sort of a gift and a curse.

One afternoon my mother walked into my bedroom with a weighted expression. I pretended not to see her and buried my face into my notebook. Normally, whenever she saw me trapped inside of my imagination, she would leave me be, but not this time. She sat on the edge of my bed and playfully tapped my head. *I hope this isn't another sex talk.* It wasn't, but she sure dropped a megabomb on me. She said it was time I met my father! *Huh?! What?! Come again?!* I'd waited for this opportunity for years, but I was very reluctant when it finally presented itself. From an emotional standpoint, my father was dead to me. I'd forced myself to believe I was fine without him. I'd built a wall around my heart that only God could tear down. My mother continued to talk, but all I heard was fear giggling within my heart.

Did she orchestrate the meeting, or had my father requested to see me? I didn't know, but it was time to face the unknown. Even though I'd pegged him as the source of most my pain, in a way, I still wanted him to be impressed. I felt the same butterflies in my stomach that I felt before playing a football game. How could someone I didn't even know have such an impact on how I felt? When my mother left the room, I stared at my notebook. My creative juices were nonexistent. My place of peace was disturbed. To me, my father's name was synonymous with a dark cloud or a poisonous weed that lived off the destruction of others. The vibe in our apartment was different that night. And I knew my mom felt it too. How long did she battle with organizing that moment? For years, my mother kept a firm grip on how her rose blossomed through the concrete, but this was outside of her control. I closed my notebook and stood in front of my bedroom mirror. *Let's get this over with.*

A handshake? Really? That was the gesture my father offered me the first, and only, time we ever met. I analyzed him from head to toe. I was his spitting image. I'd hoped the encounter would give me a sense of belonging, but it didn't. I tried to give him the benefit of the doubt and rationalize the twelve years of his absence, but he too had lived in Brooklyn that whole time. Even though Brooklyn is big enough to be occupied by over two million residents, the realization that my father had been only a train ride away was beyond disappointing. I hung with him for four days. He'd meet me and take me into his world. He lived in a basement apartment with his girlfriend at the time. I walked inside and heard a baby crying in the distance. Moments later, his girlfriend walked out holding an infant. I instantly knew the baby was my sister. I'd been on the earth for twelve years, and before my father tried to reconcile with me, he'd created another life. Well, in that four-day span, his girlfriend kicked him out, and he was living by himself in a homeless shelter. On the fourth and final day I saw him, he was unpacking his belongings into a room the size of a jail cell. I guess such is life.

During those four days, my conversations with him lacked depth and substance. I didn't know what to expect, but I wasn't particularly proud to be his son. To me, he was a defeated shell of a man with no real purpose or clear vision. In my eyes, my father was a coward, and I'd concluded that all he could ever teach me was how not to be, what not to be, and who not to be. If he wanted to know me, he was going to have to work for it. I was only twelve years old, but I was determined to be better than him. It boggled my mind that someone as educated, and accomplished as my mother would've even allowed a person of his stature the time of day. He obviously had been a different person when they first met. Surely, she must have believed he had potential and all that. But alas, if they hadn't met, I wouldn't be here sharing my story you.

I refused to be imprisoned by my thoughts. The odds were stacked against my mom and I, and the kid had to become more than just a shoulder for her to lean on. Sitting around the house praying for a miracle was no longer an option. I had to put in the work and help out financially, which meant leaving the nest. When it came to indulging in criminal activity, there was no age limit. Any and every kind of hustle was right there in the city, and whatever I wanted to become in that regard was just outside of my window. I saw teenagers with knots of money in their pockets with jaded aspirations of one day turning a rock of cocaine into a brick. Movies like *Scarface* intensified the urge to get rich by any means necessary, and some within the community embraced that notion like the eleventh commandment. Most of the young hustlers didn't live long enough to fulfill Scarface's dreams of world domination. Some didn't even live long enough to get a driver's license. But for the handful who did? They became short-lived street legends.

The gangsterization of America swooped down into poverty-stricken communities and influenced the minds of most kids. Hip-hop was in full effect, and having a gold rope chain, three-finger ring, pair of Adidas, and Panasonic two-tape cassette boom box was the shit! Hip-hop music was the artistic expression I craved, but part of the hip-hop lifestyle came with big price tags. We all loved the music, but mostly, only the drug dealers could afford to actually look the part. For me, the fast lifestyle it took to achieve the look was beneath me. My mother put in the work, time, and love to nurture those invaluable thoughts of self-worth. I knew at a young age that nothing in this world comes easy and all that glitters isn't gold. A person's character is judged by how he or she deals with adversity, and how I dealt with my mother's financial struggles was a test of sorts. In my eyes, my father had failed his test of fatherhood when he abandoned us. So, instead of succumbing to the stereotypical ways of making a dollar in my hood, I found my first job as a pizza delivery boy. It was far from glamorous, and the pay was lousy, but it felt good to make my mother proud and pass my first test of survival all by my lonesome.

Working as a pizza delivery boy broadened my landscape. On my bicycle, I delivered pizzas all over our neighborhood, traveling beyond the boundaries set by my mother. As I pedaled my ten-speed past the local drug dealers draped in jewelry, commandeering flashy cars, I knew that one day I too would taste the spoils of luxury. The fire to prove my true worth to the world became an obsession. I guess I could partly credit my father for that part of my ambition, but I've never heard of a superhero thanking the villain for his superpowers. As a pizza delivery boy, it would take me weeks to save up and purchase what a drug dealer could buy in five minutes. But I was always more intrigued with the marathon of life, not the sprint. I had that same approach with my love for acting and my dreams of making it big in Hollywood. It was always about the marathon, never the sprint.

The zoned high school near where I lived at the time didn't provide the curriculum I needed to pursue my dreams as an actor, so I applied to the Fiorello H. LaGuardia School of the Performing Arts located in Manhattan, and upon my acceptance, I became one of the only two students accepted from Community School in District 13. Some of the greatest actors and entertainers of past generations have attended the school. The path there was laid, and all I had to do was put in the work. The school is a public institution, but you couldn't just enroll. You had to be chosen through an audition process. My mother encouraged me to apply to other schools just in case I wasn't accepted, but I was confident. All my life I'd watched her teach middle school during the days, work after school, take graduate classes at night, do community service on weekends, and attend church on Sundays. So how couldn't I have absorbed her teachings and deliver on demand when necessary? My mom embodied resilience, confidence, and strength, and it was only right that I took the baton and ascended to new heights, because I stood on the shoulders of a giant.

When I first visited LaGuardia High School, I was in awe. The building was brand new. As a matter of fact, some of it was still under construction. I knew I'd made the right choice when my mom and I walked inside. I felt like my destiny was awaiting me behind those stage doors, and I couldn't think of anyone else in the world I'd have wanted to share that moment with except for her. I bet everything on making it into LaGuardia, and I was determined to make her proud. After my audition, she asked me if I thought I would be accepted, and without blinking I replied verbatim, "There's no way I didn't make it into that school!" She just grinned at the fact that her kid was a tad cocky. I used to wonder if my father possessed the same confidence as me, but after meeting him, I knew the answer to that question. It was finally time for me to blaze my own trail.

Around this time, one night I was awakened by a bloodcurdling scream. I rushed to the bathroom to find my mother leaning over the bathtub, covered in blood, crying for help. My mind raced with every scenario that could have caused the dreadful sight, and it was up to me to help save her life. Though she'd drilled me on what to do in the event of an emergency, I'd never felt so scared in my life. I ran to the phone, dialed

911, and that's when everything slowed down. Literally. Her eyes pierced through my soul. She tried to speak, but she barely had enough energy to breathe. I followed the instructions the 911 operator gave and waited for an ambulance to arrive. The thought of my mother dying in my arms was beyond terrifying. Life was teaching me a massive lesson—that death can knock on anyone's door at any given moment. Up until that point in my existence, my mom was my superwoman, my superhero. But on that night, I was introduced to Bonnie, the woman, daughter, and sister. In that very moment, I realized that even she was just a human being like everyone else on this planet.

She was unconscious by the time the paramedics banged on the door. They tried to remove me from the scene, but I refused to budge. I watched helplessly as they placed her limp body onto the stretcher. My mother was always on the go and full of energy, so to see her lying motionless diminished my soul in that moment. My very foundation was crumbling, and I'd never felt so scared in my life. One of the paramedics asked if there was another parent I could call, but the look on my face answered that question quickly. Within minutes, IV tubes hung from her arm, and agony snatched us both by the collar. On the bumpy ride to the hospital, I wanted and needed answers, but the paramedics didn't know what had caused such a massive amount of blood loss. My everything was clinging on for dear life, but the paramedics went about it as business as usual. I guess to them she was just another patient on their night shift.

When we arrived at the hospital, I trailed closely behind the paramedics as they pushed my mother into the emergency room. The doors opened, and the doctor gave us a look of exasperation. He was clearly leaving for the night having completed his shift, and my mom's life-or-death situation must've ruined whatever plans he had awaiting him after work. Fifteen minutes later, the doctor diagnosed her with a massive nosebleed brought on by blood vessels in her head that ruptured due to low blood pressure. He stuffed her nostrils with medicated gauze, and nudged me on the shoulder, but the blood flow didn't stop. They escorted us back to the ambulance, and we headed back to our apartment as if all was well.

While I braced myself for the ambulance's uncomfortable ride back home, I held her hand and prayed to God that she be healed. Suddenly, my mom jumped up as if a bolt of lightning had struck her, and she viciously tried to unhook herself from the gurney. While the paramedics tried to restrain her, she yelled at them to let her go. Nothing could calm her down, and the paramedics were literally fighting with her. When we arrived in front of our building, she broke free and jumped out of the ambulance. She ran up the stairs to our building, slipped, and fell, breaking her ankle in the process. Then she fainted. She was then rushed back to the hospital, and the new diagnosis was far from a severe nosebleed. Because the previous doctor was rushing to end his shift, he'd misdiagnosed the severity of the situation, and she'd almost died.

As I waited for hours by my mother's side, I held her hand and watched her sleep. What would my life be without her? A feeling of seriousness came over me that I'd never felt before. Up until that point, I'd lived my life pretty much carefree and careful. But as I watched my blanket of total security lying on that hospital bed, I found out how treacherous and unpredictable life really could be. Yet another lesson my father wasn't there to brace me for.

CHAPTER 2

Brooklyn's Own

The father of the righteous will greatly rejoice; he who fathers
a wise son will be glad in him.
—Proverbs 23:24 (American Standard Version)

As I matured, I began to realize the neighborhood I called home was actually a purposely constructed dumping ground for the people that mainstream society would deem the have-nots. My mother wasn't well educated and working two jobs just to be deemed a have-not. She'd put in the work and made the necessary sacrifices for the betterment of herself, me, and our family. Through rappers like KRS-One, my eyes were opened to the diabolical plans in motion that were slowly destroying our culture. My voyage for the truth was born, and I began to wonder how society's social classes were created. I knew certain conditions existed way before my conception, but why hadn't anyone other than my mom sat me down to really explain the ways of the world? Once again, hip-hop would provide me with the lessons my father didn't provide.

A mother's love is infinite, but during those crucial adolescent years, I needed a father to teach me how to evolve from a boy to a man, from the most complicated things, like how to physically defend myself, to the most simple of things, like how to shave. There comes a time in every boy's life when he needs a man's advice to help him make certain transitions. See, when a mother says everything is going to be all right, she means it wholeheartedly, but there is more of an emotional connotation.

I knew my mom would do all that she could, and I felt an obligation to help in the ways that I could as well. But when an active father says everything's going to be all right, it's not suggestive. There isn't a soft undertone but rather a confirmation that he'll die trying to make everything be all right. Not to say any mother wouldn't do the same, but God made men and women different for a reason. Just as in the animal kingdom, a male's job is to protect and provide. And before all of you women reading this break out your feminist armor, believe and trust that I'm all about gender equality and such. But hey, I guess I'm old-school when it comes to certain things, and I believe it's a man's job to protect and provide for his family.

My father didn't have to be in a relationship with my mom or shower me with gifts, but he could've at least tried to provide something, anything but absence. I mean, at some point in the past he'd loved my mom, right? As children we all want to believe that our parents conceived us out of love, but I began to think maybe he had ulterior motives with my mother in that regard. Maybe I was just the product of him trying to save and control his relationship with her. Since he never took the time with me to explain his side of the coin, in my mind, those possibilities were endless. So naturally, he took the blame for every struggle we endured. My mother's near-death experience opened up the floodgates of maturity for me, and I haven't quite looked at life the same since.

In '88, I auditioned for and got a role in an NYU student film entitled *The Green Flash*. It ended up getting nominated for an award at the Chicago International Film Festival. It was a shoestring, super-low-budget film, but it was also the beginnings of my pursuit of happiness, the first step in my journey to becoming a professional actor. I was only fifteen years old, yet there I was already on the road to fulfilling my dreams. Though it was just an NYU student film, the experience of filming *The Green Flash* made me feel like I was no longer just wishing upon a star. At such a young age, it felt like I'd found my purpose, and I'd sometimes wonder, what was my father's excuse for having not done so for himself at that point? The character I played in the film was an orphan who bounced around from shelter to shelter with little to no hope. I was so immersed into the experience that I didn't even see the connection that was so starkly obvious. The character I played not only reflected my father's reality—an unstable life filled with little hope—but was also fatherless himself.

The Fiorello H. LaGuardia School of the Performing Arts gave me hope. I was constantly surrounded by brimming creativity. Every day I walked the same hallways that the groundbreaking movie *Fame* was based on. LaGuardia was literally where my dreams first began to come alive outwardly. I was fueled to pursue my passion even harder, and I developed a no-nonsense attitude when it came to achieving my goals. That new attitude shortened a few friendships back in my neighborhood, but I was dedicated to changing my family's tomorrows. My mom never put any pressure on me to be a provider; it was all self-inflicted due to the absence of my father. I felt as if I was the only man in her life who truly cared. And I willingly embraced that role.

I saw firsthand how a lack of vision and self-worth could lead someone down a destructive path. In my mind, I was genetically 50 percent my father. So would self-destruction happen to me by default? Would I ultimately end up living in a room no bigger than a jail cell and have a fruitless relationship with my children? Fears can imprison one's mind for sure. I had no aspirations of being anything like him, but at that age, the fears of such attempted to haunt my thoughts. Had I expressed my fears, I'm sure my mother would've given me the right words to dispel that burning insecurity. But I didn't need comforting words; I needed my father to be more than just a rolling stone and a sower of seeds. I could've dealt with him living in unstable conditions and raising other children, but not being an honorable man was unforgivable in my eyes.

I didn't have thoughts of celebrating having gotten into LaGuardia. To me, it was merely the first step on my journey toward greatness. The school was in Manhattan, which was an hour away from where I lived, and "the city"—the epicenter of New York's hustle and bustle—was very different. At LaGuardia competition was everywhere, and at any moment your classmate could land a job on a television series or a feature film. Playing football had sharpened my competitive nature, but acting required a completely different set of skills. In football, I was faster, stronger, and smarter than some of my opponents. But none of that mattered in the world of acting. How do you bring life to a character you've never met? How do you harness your life's experiences and plunge into the emotional abyss of your own reality? Since I was a child, the poems and short stories I wrote helped me to escape. Constantly moving into different neighborhoods gave me a skill to ingest the nuances of details very quickly and then detach. And growing up lower middle class and fatherless gave me the urgency to prosper. Those are some of the life ingredients that I'm built from. Though I wouldn't recommend that combination of ingredients in order to become a successful actor, in hindsight, those ingredients showed themselves to be beneficial to the foundation of my achievements.

During this time, my desire of having a James Evans in the household had become a thing of the past. *The Cosby Show* had emerged, and Cliff Huxtable was born. He was a protector and provider—a stern but funny, very loving, successful father. The Huxtables lived in a beautiful brownstone in Brooklyn, and they were the first black family on television that represented more than hope. They actually had a slice of the American pie. In the hood, it seemed like we only lived to complain about another day. The phrase "I'm just tryin' to make a dollar outta' fifteen cents" became an excuse to take shortcuts. I was once again glued to my television screen, wondering why my mother hadn't yet found her Cliff Huxtable. Just like Claire Huxtable, my mom was strong, smart, beautiful, and goal oriented. As far as I was concerned, my mom was the perfect catch and worthy of a successful man.

After the success of *The Cosby Show*, black men who masqueraded behind "the white man is holding us down" philosophy became irrelevant really. In my opinion, there's no difference between a black man waiting for a handout and a stingy, self-entitled white man. They're both counterproductive. Of course at the time, black men still struggled like hell in America, but even if just for fictional purposes, *The Cosby Show* raised the bar as to what we could achieve. To me, Cliff Huxtable represented the power of making the right choices. He didn't just represent a father in the home; he also represented hard work having led to accomplishing one's goals. See, though I have a deep admiration for those who lived through the black power movement of the late '60s, like my mother, I wasn't alive to personally witness it. For my generation, *The Cosby Show* will forever be a positive reflection of black culture. It truly made us feel proud to be black, and it helped lead to my decision not to dwell on the past pains of our people but rather on how to improve our communities in the now. *The Cosby Show* did much more than make us laugh; it moved us light-years beyond the blaxploitation films of days past. To that degree, that's why the issues surrounding Bill Cosby today completely broke my heart. It's like an integral piece of my childhood died.

I made a choice to avoid negativity as best I could and to remove myself from those who didn't vibrate on the same plane of energy as I did. I applauded the character James Evans for his resilience, but looking back, he did more bickering and jive talking than job hunting. I wondered if my father had fallen victim to the same and was simply waiting for his forty acres and a mule instead of making the proper choices to prosper, like my choices to be a pizza delivery boy and then sell sneakers at the Athlete's Foot instead of becoming a drug dealer. Those choices saved my mother thousands of dollars in bail money or, even worse, funeral arrangements. Even at that age, I understood the power of choice. *The Cosby Show*'s intellectual way of making those points gave me clarity. Emotionally, there was a bittersweet victory for me in those lessons, because no kid wants to be deemed a choice. They just want to be loved unconditionally. But if I was merely a mistake for my father, that burden would fall on his soul, not mine. *The Cosby Show* proudly and unapologetically displayed the blueprint of what a family could be when generational fatherlessness is prevented. And if just for that moment, black society at large was awakening from its slumber when it came to the issue.

At LaGuardia, we had the freedom to express ourselves artistically, but that atmosphere also fueled the illusion that we were all equally matched in that regard. In reality, only a few of us would actually be fortunate enough to bring our dreams to fruition. My mom taught me the only difference between a dreamer and a doer is their work ethic. And I would not be outworked. As a freshman from the streets of Brooklyn, I exuded a certain type of confidence. I partly credit that type of braggadocio to the rapper Big Daddy Kane. Of course there were many others, but Kane was from Brooklyn like me, and us young dudes from the borough embodied his boisterous swag. His music taught me how to conduct myself in my young adult life, especially with the girls. Having grown up in a family full of women, it was natural for me to be surrounded by them. At LaGuardia, it was no different. Maybe it was my high-top fade or my cooler-than-a-fan demeanor, but when you mix in all of that with male adolescent hormones, you get the recipe for what most teenage boys go through.

Marlon Wayans attended LaGuardia as well, so his name rang through the hallways. At that time, I didn't know anything about him except we sort of didn't like each other. See, back in the late '70s, the movie *Rocky* was a phenomenon. It had me, along with lots of other kids, wanting to be a boxer, or at least to train like one. So, during my freshman year at LaGuardia, I used to walk the hallways bouncing a small blue handball just like Rocky did. One day my ball went missing, and I thought Marlon and his friends took it. I approached him, and we exchanged some heated words. We were supposed to have this big showdown after school, but that never happened. Next thing I know, we're in the same drama class. A couple of weeks later, our drama teacher made us scene partners. I figured that wasn't going to work, because we all know that boys will be boys. One thing led to another, and one day during a scene rehearsal, Marlon and I got into a physical altercation. Our wrestling match lasted a few minutes. We realized we ranked the same in that sense. That defining moment turned our dislike for one another into a mutual respect, and it is the foundation of what is still to this day a powerful, lifelong brotherhood.

By sophomore year, Marlon introduced me to a younger classman named Mitch. By then the Wayans' family name was on fire from the hit comedy movie *I'm Gonna Git You Sucka*. While a lot of people at LaGuardia flocked around Marlon because of his older brother's success, that film was the spark that lit his desire to create his own lane. By that time, my mom and I had moved to Queens, and it just so happened that Mitch lived not too far from me. He helped me learn the transit system in Queens, and our brotherhood bloomed from there. I introduced Marlon and Mitch to my other boys G and Jeff, who were also from Queens. And just like that, the crew was born!

The bond of brotherhood I developed with these guys was in every way a divine order. Marlon's parents were married and raised their ten kids in the Chelsea projects in Lower Manhattan. Mitch had lost both of his parents as a child, but his aunt and uncle-in-law filled that void as best they could. Jeff's pop was an active father even though his parents weren't together. And G was fatherless like me. God surrounded me with these incredible brothers, and we challenged one another to constantly be our best selves. Whenever we spoke about the adversities of our lives, we rarely dwelled on the negatives. Instead, we'd focus on the positives and swim in appreciation of our individual situations. I mean, quite frankly, fatherlessness was normal in the hood. Sadly, it still is today. As men, we're trained to sweep our vulnerabilities under the rug, and that's what we did. Whenever we had one of our infamous roasting sessions, Marlon would always joke by pointing out a homeless man on the street and asking, "Is that your father?" We'd all burst into laughter, and Marlon would win another round. I never took it personally, because those types of jokes just made me come back harder. When my boys and I weren't joking or chasing girls, perfecting our crafts was our number one priority. We each possessed a certain hunger that gave us an edge. We were just different from the norm.

We all grew up in different family circumstances, but one thing we had in common was our emotional connection to hip-hop. Your knowledge of the culture determined how real you were, and we knew it to the fullest. We were the generation of the '70s that hip-hop raised. And just when we thought the culture couldn't teach us anymore, something very special happened. Hailing from Long Island, a new rapper emerged and shifted the culture immensely. His name was Rakim. Even though Rakim was only five years older than me, he dropped knowledge like an old wise man from deep in the bushes of Jamaica. He embodied the teachings of KRS-One, had N.W.A.'s street edge, and exuded Big Daddy Kane's swag.

I would sometimes wonder if he'd had an active father in his life who'd instilled those lessons within him or if he'd grown up fatherless, like most of the kids in the hoods of New York. Hip-hop was taking fatherless boys through their voyage into manhood, and Rakim was the epitome of that evolution. He taught us that going along with whatever was trending, just because, was a dangerous thing to do. And his deep, philosophical lyrics sparked the leader within all of us.

In 1990, my senior year, the struggle between a single mother and her teenage son brought about situations that only an alpha male could control. But who was going to control me? Who'd earned that right? No man, at that point, really had those qualifications. I developed a new attitude: if you weren't with me, you were against me. And if you didn't know what side you were on, I had no problem reminding you of which one. Though I was still a happy teenager for the most part, deep inside of my mind, a bitterness was festering. We were the generation that society was afraid of. We were rebellious, and knowledge of self reigned supreme. Fortunately, my mom's teachings kept me in line, but back then, every teenager in the hoods of Brooklyn was one decision away from being in some real trouble.

Having skipped a grade in elementary school, I was only sixteen years old when I finished my time at LaGuardia. I was laser focused on my goals but faced with the reality of having to go to college and find a job. Even though my mom supported me as best she could, realistically, being a working actor was a super rocky road filled with a variety of land mines. Shortly thereafter, I received information for a casting opportunity for a movie called *Juice*. The first person I called was my mother. I guess you could say she was a tad bit excited, but I'm sure if I'd told her I was accepted into a historical black college, she would've screamed at the top of her lungs! For years, she'd heard me talk of the day I would land a starring role in a movie. So to her, it was probably just more talk of the same. Not that she knew enough about the entertainment biz to know that the chances of me actually getting a starring role in a movie were slim to none. I mean, I guess it's like when Tom Brady told his parents his dream was to one day play in the NFL, right? Like who knew? Regardless of what anyone thought, the universe heard my wishes and gave me the opportunity to prove all the statistics and naysayers wrong. Needless to say, I got the role. And I knew that opportunity was going to propel me to new heights.

Like most people, I was under the impression that when you landed a starring role in a movie, you got rich overnight. Glitz and glamor, right? No. Not at all. While filming *Juice*, I wasn't chauffeured to the set or pampered in some luxurious trailer. I was on the train like everyone else. And on one of the first days of shooting, Hollywood taught me an extremely brutal and sobering lesson, and that's that the show must go on. While I was trying to level up in my life, I saw someone else's end too soon. We filmed *Juice* up in the bowels of Harlem. One day on set, there was a dead body lying right in front of the building we were filming in. Burgundy bloodstains seeped through the white sheet that covered the corpse. Just another day in the hood, right? I instantly thought filming for the day was over, but man, was I wrong. After twenty or so minutes of murmuring from the producers and spectators, I stood in disbelief as the camera crew grabbed their gear and basically stepped over the body as if it were a prop. The show must go on. Emotionally, my father represented that same scenario to me. While he unapologetically moved about in his life, metaphorically, I was the dead body that he constantly stepped over. Welcome to Hollywood, kid.

The premiere for *Juice* arrived, and nothing made me more proud than to have my mother by my side. Having a leading role in the movie was what I'd worked for, but on that night, I realized a much deeper accomplishment. I'd always told my mom I would make it, but that night was the moment of genuine confirmation. It was a long ways from pedaling a ten-speed through the streets of Brooklyn, being paid under the table to deliver pizza to my fellow residents. In just four years, I'd gone from a bright-eyed freshman attending the same high school as Robert De Niro and Al Pacino, to my mother and me sitting two seats away from Diana Ross at a movie premiere where I was one of the stars. Astounding! At just seventeen years old, I became, well, famous. Brooklyn's own had made it.

When the ending credits of the movie came on screen, the audience erupted into a loud cheer. Ironically, Rakim's song "Know the Ledge" accompanied the ending credits on the score of my very first feature film. Then again, that probably wasn't irony at all. As the song played, everyone bobbed their heads. To me, that divine poetry was hip-hop's way of saying, *Good job, son*. How sweet would that night have been if my father had also been there enjoying that moment along with us? It would've been the complete circle of man, woman, and child, as God intended. But honestly, I was so far removed in my heart from any connection with him that his absence made that moment even more enjoyable.

That was my first taste of fame, and the power associated with it was intoxicating. While I was still learning who I was as a human being, the public hailed me for a character I'd portrayed on the big screen. It's trippy because when I was young, I'd stare into the mirror and wonder what my father looked like. Now, he probably couldn't turn a corner without seeing my face plastered on billboards and posters all over the city. Whenever someone used to say I looked like him, I detested it. But now the tides had turned drastically. I wondered how he responded when his friends or strangers said he looked like Q from the movie *Juice*. Did he say I was his son? Did his face light up with pride, or was it shadowed in shame? Did he even see the movie? Probably so ...

As my career began to sprout, I learned about the bizarre "relationship" between fans and entertainers. It's kind of similar to the relationship between a child and an inactive parent. See, there's no true connection between a child and an inactive parent, but that child is consumed by expectations he or she feels the inactive parent should fulfill. Fans perceive their "connections" with entertainers as being authentic, but 99.9 percent of the time, those connections aren't based on any actual interactions. Unless fans were to spend continued, quality time with the human being behind the title of entertainer, they won't truly know who or how that person really is. Before I met my father, I had a preconceived idea of how I wanted our relationship to be. Even in the midst of fathoms of doubt, I naturally wanted to be his fan. When my assumption of what our relationship should've been didn't deliver itself, I was beyond disappointed, and there was no room for his redemption in my eyes. After dealing with the public's fascination with the character Q, the world that used to seem so big to me became so much smaller. I needed a space just to be my natural self and come down from the clouds of adulation. I entrusted my boys with that responsibility, and I must say, I feel like they did a damn good job. We never allowed each other to forget who we truly were as human beings at our cores.

Responsible parents control their kids' fascination with entertainers and athletes just by limiting their access to technology, and they give their children the tools to build fruitful lives of their own, instead of just admiring the fruitful lives of others. Too many parents have allowed society to dictate who's a proper role model for their kids. Stylishly dunking a basketball doesn't make you a role model, just a great basketball player. Every parent must step in and control how such information is being fed to these young, impressionable minds. A great sports figure or entertainer is just a one-dimensional being when compared to active parents. Kids love popular sports figures and entertainers when they're at the pinnacle of their success, but every kid also loves his or her parents organically just as they are. Fathers must embrace the influential, powerful roles they've been given. When a son watches his father put on a pair of shoes, he mimics his every move, and he stands by his father's shoulder to see if he's grown an inch taller.

Through the glamorization of entertainers and athletes, society at large has lost sight of the biggest stars on the planet: parents. Millions of people tune in to watch athletes and entertainers walk to a podium and humbly accept their awards. And? The first person they all usually thank is their mother. It's alarmingly imbalanced how many stars thank their mothers versus their fathers after receiving an award. Just something for you to ponder on … They're thanking these women for having scraped together pennies just to pay the rent, for having gotten up every morning and sacrificed themselves just so their children could learn to follow their dreams of becoming the next Sean Combs or Serena Williams. My mother was no different. She couldn't help me to learn my lines for a movie role or give me advice on what my character's emotional journey was, just like I'm pretty sure Drake's mom never gave him advice on how to spit a hot sixteen. But our mothers—mine, Drake's, and a myriad of others—made it possible for us to truly entertain the thoughts of exploring our artistic dreams and bringing them to reality. So, while the public was admiring roles that I'd played, I was admiring my mother for giving me the opportunity to dream big. She was the one who truly deserved the red-carpet treatment.

In the early '90s, the fatherless generation of the '70s started to become fathers themselves. For some, the cycle of fatherlessness would repeat. When an active father has done his job, at some point, he has to simply trust the guidance he's instilled into his kids. To a certain degree, hip-hop did the same, but did it truly prepare us to be effective parents or not? Hip-hop had walked us through our childhood into our teenage years and taught us about our self-worth, rich heritage, and staunch pride, as well as cold-blooded violence, reckless indulgence of drugs, and inconsequential, meaningless sex. It had also helped to trick us into believing the word *nigga* was a term of endearment and the word *bitch* was how you defined a woman you desired.

Rappers of the previous decades became grandparents to the culture, and eventually some faded away into the sunset. And so hip-hop itself would embrace a whole new generation of fatherless children while watching my generation from a close distance. New musical father figures were born, and at times, those figures appeared to be too immature to handle their responsibilities to the culture. We were way too young to take ourselves seriously, and it was literally one big party at all times, at all costs. We danced until our clothes were drenched in sweat, and the goal was to find a pretty girl to have sex with by the night's end. Art truly imitates life, and ours at the time gave active parents an up-close view of our generation. But still, it was all masked behind one word: *entertainment*.

One group that would take a much more serious approach musically was Ed O.G. & Da Bulldogs. They released a powerful song called "Be a Father to Your Child." This song not only struck a chord with me personally but also showed the world that hip-hop culture could take a bold and responsible stance against fatherlessness. Up until that point, I'd accepted the issue as something we never really addressed in the culture. That song brought the issue to the forefront in a way that the hood could understand.

Another fatherless product of hip-hop was the legend himself, Tupac Shakur. He tackled many tough issues in his music, especially those that impacted our communities. Of course we both starred in the classic film *Juice*, and we got to know one another well. One day Pac invited me to hang out at his mother's apartment. Afeni Shakur was a very strong, smart, and lovely woman. While we chilled out talking, listening to music, Pac started to roll a blunt right there in front of his mom. Such a scenario was extremely unfamiliar to me, but it helped me to understand the type of environment he'd experienced growing up. The night that Tupac passed on, hours before they'd announced it on the news and radio, he came to me in a dream. He told me that I had to choose a side. We had this belief between one another which was the political system in our country were essentially offense and defense, but playing for the same team. Young rebellious minds, call it what you want. I used to think that was what he was referring to, but now I know he was telling me something much deeper. He was giving me a beneficial jewel I'd be able to carry throughout my life. Ultimately, no one can live on both sides of any fence. One has to make choices and stand by their convictions.

One of Tupac's songs, "Brenda's Got a Baby," depicted a vivid picture of the pitfalls associated with teenage pregnancy. I remember the impact that musical masterpiece had on the culture at the time. Even though it's stood the test of time, it didn't resonate enough with certain men for them to change their actions regarding their own issues surrounding parenthood. And I know for a fact that was Pac's intent when he wrote the song—to spark those flames of change.

Since I was seven years old, hip-hop taught me all about life. But it seems that now, some three-minute song isn't enough for this newer generation. Has the commercialization of our music, and in effect our culture, forever ruined its foundation? Think about that ... Because the notion insinuates that the blind began leading the blind. Crime rates rose, as did single-parent households headed up by women. And after all we'd been through? After all the historic information we'd learned from leaders like Malcolm X? After all the oppressive agendas we'd been informed about from activists like Dick Gregory? After all the messages we'd received from our musical prophets like Bob Marley? How could it be? Well, the answer is simple. Films like the classic *New Jack City* would go on to be akin to the black *Scarface*. *New Jack City* was heavily influenced by the hip-hop culture, but it was also very influential to a large demographic within the culture itself. Now, of course I'm not blaming *New Jack City*. I loved the film my damn self! I'm simply pointing out some of the themes and messages it transmitted. Through hip-hop, yeah, we learned the game of life, but we never really learned to cherish simplicity, nor the dynamics of a traditional family structure. We didn't know how to treat our women with respect. So how are we supposed to lead ourselves in the future? This new generation could really use the teachings of Rakim and a host of others. But it seems like the business of hip-hop isn't into uplifting anymore; it's all about the money now.

Juice gave me fame, but I was exponentially far from being rich. After having paid agent fees, taxes, and lawyer fees, I walked away with roughly $12,000. Twelve grand doesn't sound like much, but twelve grand in the hands of a teenager is definitely what we call *hood rich*. My mom urged me to open a savings and checking account, which I did. But other than her immediate recommendations, I had no one to really give me any long-term financial advice. It would've been an asset to hear a feasible, effective perspective on how to be young, flashy, and fly while avoiding certain financial pitfalls. But I was no longer just a nephew or a grandson. In my eyes, I was the new head of the household. I'd always wanted to show my friends in Brooklyn that there were other ways to make a living besides hustling drugs or whatever. My role in *Juice* was an example of that. I was an inspiration. I represented hope to my friends back on the block. And I took that position with honor, because I was proud of myself.

One day, I was driving in my brand-new BMW 325i with a pretty woman I was dating. As we rode through my old hood, I leaned back with my left hand on the steering wheel, enjoying the views of my borough. As the light turned red, I looked over to the left and saw a man standing on the corner selling CDs and incense. It was my father. Unbelievable! Normally, the traffic lights on this street changed at a swift pace, but on that day it was as if the red light took its time for me. I looked again just to make sure. No doubt—it was him. Befuddlement and shock are understatements to explain what I felt in that moment. A bunch of thoughts ran through my mind; emotions ran through my body. Here I was in a brand-new Bimmer, which made everyone who saw it stop and stare, including him. But no one could see who was behind those dark tinted windows. I stared at him in utter disbelief. Why was this moment happening? What did it mean? I turned to the woman in the passenger's seat and said, "That's my father." She looked at him and was immediately stunned. "Oh my God, you look just like him!" Then with wide eyes she asked, "Aren't you going to stop and say something?" My response? I calmly hit the gas and drove off.

Now to some, pulling over and having a conversation with him may seem like the logical thing to have done. But being that my relationship with him was nonexistent, I literally wouldn't have known what to say. I was only nineteen years old, and in the seven years since I'd last met him, I'd made a life for myself. See, ultimately life is about the choices you make, and I'd made a choice to take advantage of every minute to improve the life of my family. He had made different choices. I'm not judging anyone who may be in similar circumstances, but for me, him selling incense on the corner was a sum total of his own choices in relation to me. Honestly, I felt a sense of victory, as if that moment represented a win for all the years he'd left my mother and me out to dry.

To the public, I was now a product first, human being second. I'd experienced things that no one in my family ever had, and the road was beginning to be paved for me to gain a level of financial success that no one in my family had ever reached. The ramifications were enormous. I was far from being a parent myself, but I began to become highly aware of the familial effects caused by the generational cycle of fatherlessness in my family. I wanted my unborn kids to grow up in a family of strong, respected men. So I worked tirelessly at my craft, with goals of one day reaching the zenith in Hollywood. But I damn sure wasn't prepared to be at the top of the food chain. My boys kept me grounded, and I never second-guessed their agendas. Maybe if certain people in my life had taken the time to really get to know me when I was younger, they wouldn't have had to deal with the trust issues that came with my newfound celebrity around that time. There's a saying, "Become what you seek," and in many ways, I'd become the man I'd wished I had as a mentor. On the surface all these things just sound like mere personal accomplishments, but beneath the lights, camera, and action was a myriad of deep-rooted, unresolved issues.

Around this time, my mom remarried. She'd found her own love and life partner in Rhodine Burgess. God must've known that my Hollywood journey was going to take up the majority of my time, so he sent someone into her life to fill that void in a sense. Something about Rhodine was special. Raised on a farm in South Carolina, he'd joined the U.S. Navy as a young buck, and had traveled the world over. He was genuine, knowledgeable about cultures and life in general, and he loved my mother. I was then too old to throw footballs in the park with him, but he was a great listener, and he allowed me to open up. With all that my mother and I had endured up to that point in time, Rhodine was the exact antidote she needed for herself. Over time, I realized that he and I were kindred souls in a way. To this day, he remains an unbiased ear of reason for me. It was a relief to know that I wasn't the only alpha male source of love for my mother. I was happy her heart was full.

Now, the character Q and I shared a few similarities. That character represented many young, fatherless men in America. In hindsight, I realize the same way James Evans was designed to represent the adversities black men faced in the '70s, Q represented a new generation of young, oftentimes misguided men. I remember when I first read the script to *Juice*, the story resonated with me so deeply that it never occurred to me *why* the character didn't have a father. It's like that was so normal to me that it didn't even matter. Side note to all you aspiring actors out there: you always need to know the source of any character's pain, down to each and every detail. In this case, *why* didn't Q have his father in his life? What happened between Q's mom and dad? Sorting out such history will enable you to immerse yourself much deeper into any character you play. So, my lack of such a notion at the time shows how green I was as an actor then. Still, the four main characters in *Juice* were an exact depiction of the impact hip-hop had on fatherless kids in the hood. We four actors were all teenagers and proud to be a part of something great. But little did any of us know that we were kind of being chosen to be new role models for our generation. The same way I looked up to guys like Kane and Rakim, there were young kids who looked up to Q. But I wasn't yet mature enough to decipher the weight of that reality.

I believe it's literally a crime to leave a defenseless child among the wolves, to figure out adulthood without first having some sense of knowledge of self. How has society at large normalized the fact that there are hundreds of thousands of kids raising themselves without the proper tools and guidance from their parents? Taking a life is a brutal and horrible act, but so is a parent abandoning a life he or she helped to create. Unlike murder, fatherlessness doesn't leave a gory scene of blood or the image of a body lying lifeless. The act of fatherlessness is quiet. It happens in stealth, and the destruction left in its wake hides behind the smile of the child—or, in my case, my talent. The pain of fatherlessness often manifests itself as misguided anger, and a lot of times it's the origin of things like bullying, drug usage, and more. There is no one way to express the emptiness in one's soul associated with growing up without a father. Too many men have become emotional murderers yet still walk the streets as if they've never committed a crime. When a life is taken, society gasps and begs God to comfort the family. But fatherless children are left to mend themselves emotionally, which is akin to being a prisoner trapped in a corpse of bitterness.

Millions of people tune in to watch Maury Povich's show for one reason: to find out the results of the infamous paternity test. Why is society addicted to that type of show? Think about that for a moment. Are we so sick that we enjoy watching what's essentially the emotional demise of a fellow human being, one who's a child at that? With judgmental eyes, people wait with anticipation to see whether the man will be outed as the father or do a celebratory dance because he isn't. Maury enjoys the power of holding on to the golden envelope that contains the answer, which is really just the surface of a deeply troubling problem. Who is the father? Just before the results are read, on cue, there's a commercial break to keep the viewers in suspense. My take? How have we allowed society to turn a child's mental and emotional welfare into our personal amusement? After the break, the child's face is displayed in the background as the bearers of that innocent life scream obscenities back and forth at one another. The kid is too young to know that millions of people are watching his or her potential identity crisis unfold. "You are not the father!" The enjoyment a man expresses when he finds out he isn't the father is a bit saddening. There's something terribly wrong when finding out you're not the father of someone's child inspires the same reaction as winning the lottery. Look at how proudly the man will say, "That ain't my kid!" Music plays, and his victory dance goes viral.

What's interesting is how the fear of becoming a father apparently didn't present itself in the beginning, when the man first had sex with the woman. Is that lack of responsibility simply embedded within that person? What messages are we sending our youth who watch shows like this? Putting oneself in a position to create a life is never ever addressed, only the outcomes of such. Ultimately, these messages tell kids that it's okay to have unprotected sex and gamble with creating a human life.

I wonder if those types of shows offer assistance and counseling to help the mother and the child cope with the aftermath. Why is there so much emphasis on making a spectacle of what's essentially a jarring family crisis? Have we completely lost the desire for traditional family values? Are we too desensitized and disenfranchised to even care anymore? "She almost got me!" That's what the so-called lucky man will say among his friends. He'll live to sow another seed. But these types of shows draw us into the very problem that is destroying the fabric of this country. A problem protected by the banner of entertainment will not receive the urgency it deserves. Certain powers that be know that too, but it seems we've been rocked to sleep.

Maury's show has been around since the '90s, and nowadays, everything is public record. The Internet holds an abyss of information from past to present that is accessible at the press of a button. What I'm getting at is there are adults living today whose identity crisis was displayed on that show for the entire country to see. Imagine being able to pull up footage of some dude jumping up and down with excitement because he was not your father! Imagine seeing the disappointment and confusion on your mother's face when she realizes she doesn't know who she laid with to conceive you. Even worse, imagine seeing some dude's regret because he *is* your biological father. Does anyone besides me think about these types of things?!

Now, everyone deserves redemption, but how do you forgive an adult who refuses to love his or her own child? What type of impact does that have on a kid's sense of worth? The phrase "I never asked to be here" is occasionally used in a sarcastic manner, but there are many layers to that statement. There are generations of children whose parents never intended on becoming a family to begin with. Even though my father didn't put in the time, work, or effort, I refused to believe I was just a by-product of his mistake. As long as we find humor in that type of pain and turn the dynamics of a broken home into our amusement, the problem will persist and, dare I say, continue to flourish. Which generation will no longer accept this as normalcy?

CHAPTER 3

Know the Ledge

And that ye be kind to your parents. Whether one or both of them attain old age, say not to them a word of contempt, nor repel them, but address them in terms of honor.

—Koran 17:23–25

D r. Martin Luther King Jr. The name alone is a thousand-page book, but to his own children he was simply Dad. While the world rallied behind his loving ideologies of peace and equality for all, he also represented fatherhood. Way before fictitious characters like James Evans and Cliff Huxtable, there was MLK. He had the nation's ears, and he was the most influential black man in America of that time. Leaders like MLK only come once in a lifetime, and we really don't have the luxury to wait for another to fill his shoes. Most certainly don't possess the same amount of courage and conviction as he did, but still we must seize our own personal potential to lead with such eloquence and strength. We must get a grasp on the myriad of disconcerting issues in our society and make it our mission to change them. With his words and resilience, MLK changed the social climate in America forever. He saw a problem, and he dedicated his life to fixing it.

On Christmas Eve in '68, eight months after the assassination of MLK, the King family appeared on the show *60 Minutes*. It was to be the family's first Christmas without their beloved patriarch. During the interview, the host asked one of Dr. King's sons who he wanted to be when he grew up. The seven-year-old boy replied, "I want to be a preacher like my father." I imagine it wasn't until he grew older that he understood being a preacher only scratched the surface of what his father meant to the world. MLK was a man who was martyred for the progress and prosperity of people much like myself. If you're a father and you were to die today, what remembrances would you leave behind for your children to forever cherish? If all you leave behind is monetary goods, you've left nothing but material. MLK left much more than that to his children. He left an everlasting legacy of love, bravery, and sacrifice. He left the blueprint for how to influence society to be at its best. He left the pieces to a vision that we all must rebuild. We must resurrect the priceless value of fatherhood and family to truly change the world in the ways MLK intended.

All kids should dream for and pursue a life better than the one their parents lived prior to them. And as parents, sometimes we have to be fueled by the love of our children to overcome our personal demons. Apparently, my father must not have possessed the dogged determination needed to change himself for my betterment, but I was the exact opposite. At the age of twenty-one, God decided it was time for me to change my world for the betterment of my little sister, Aisha. The universe knew that our father's style of absentee parenting would ultimately be toxic to her. And so, in yet another example of divine poetry, I was able to locate my sister. And everything I believed about my father was confirmed once more. I immediately knew I would have to become her example of a father's love. I didn't want her to grow up with the same emotional voids that I'd grown up with. I couldn't accept her festering with an innate hatred toward men. I wouldn't accept her evolving into a woman whose life's baggage was filled to the brim with daddy issues. The last time I'd seen her, she was only six weeks old, and now she was eleven. I knew she was too young to comprehend much of our family issues, but I made a vow to myself to love and protect her no matter what uncharted waters lay ahead.

The more we connected, the more I had to mentally deal with the reality of our father's continued failure to think of someone other than himself. I guess subconsciously I'd hoped he would've taken the birth of his daughter as a second chance at becoming a better man, but I was wrong. Whenever I visited her, he was never once there. The crazy part is he only lived a few blocks down the street from where she lived at the time. Her mom had her own personal struggles, so Aisha lived with her aunt, for whom I have an immense respect and admiration.

More times than not, when a girl grows up fatherless, she ends up seeking the wrong type of attention from men and becomes promiscuous. And that's because she's seeking the attention and love she never received from her father. In my years, that's only shown itself to be a recipe for disaster. No matter who it is, the coldhearted streets will always win, and that innocent little girl turned woman becomes physical fodder for the masses. Women have to deal with a very different set of emotions from us men with regard to growing up fatherless. All I knew was that Aisha would have me for the rest of her life. It was my duty to become the father figure that she never had.

The comedic genius Chris Rock made a profound statement about fatherhood during one of his performances. He said whenever a father boasts about taking care of his kids, people's response should be "You're supposed to take care of your kids." As factual as that statement is, we must keep in mind that many fathers, who themselves grew up fatherless, look for affirmation of a job done well. Does wanting a pat on the back for doing what you're ideally supposed to do lower the value of your actions? For my salt, the answer is relative. We can't negate the history of cycles that created such a train of thought. We have to make the issue a continuous trending topic of discussion, because a fatherless child affects us all. From an ethical standpoint, society needs to truly recognize the rampant, negative impacts of fatherlessness that reverberate across all communities, rich and poor alike.

Taking in my sister gave me somewhat of an idea of what it takes to be a father figure. When the man who is obligated to love his child fails to even be present, that child's perception of love is tainted, sometimes forever. I was ten years older than my sister, and in certain moments when we spent time together, an awkward silence would fall between us. She was very shy. *Is it me?* I'd wonder. *Am I doing this big brother thing right?*

When she was of age to have more-mature conversations, my career was then taking me around the world. We still kept in touch of course, but how much of an impact could a big brother have on his little sister over the phone? I realized she was part of the new generation of fatherless children, which hip-hop had also taken in. I knew how the culture had influenced me as a youngin', but this was the first time I'd really considered the domino effects the culture could have on a young, fatherless woman. Whenever I was back home in New York, I always made time to see her. I was aspiring to be a good big brother to my teenage sister. At times, I sensed my celebrity might've been intimidating to her, and I dealt with that in my own way. There were many layers I had to peel back so she could know she was always just dealing with her brother, Omar, and not the celebrity people stopped in the streets to ask for an autograph while we walked to the store.

We were now smack-dab in the midst of what is widely considered the golden era of hip-hop. Groups like A Tribe Called Quest fed the airwaves with positive vibes, while other groups like the Wu-Tang Clan and Mobb Deep fed us more rudimentary and explicit stories of survival. And of course there were the Mount Rushmore titans of the culture, Biggie, Jay-Z, and Nas. Their poetic messages were powerful and had gravitas. Compared to the artists of the early '80s, our generation gave a much deeper and more graphic perspective on the happenings of life in the hood. It amazed me how so many fatherless children shared this artistic connection. I expressed myself through music as well, but as the laws of the universe would have it, acting was the platform I was bestowed with.

Around '93, basketball legend Charles Barkley came under fire for stating in a TV commercial, "I am not a role model." Even though he didn't sing or rap, he was speaking for all genres of entertainment with this earth-shattering statement. In many ways, it's not the entertainment industry's concern to raise your children. It's interesting because being that musicians essentially sell a lifestyle through their music, a rapper can't really say, "What I rap about isn't real." Rappers need your kids to believe their words are valid and true. Yet time and time again, when rappers get locked up, put on trial, and have their own lyrics used against them in a court of law, their lawyers always sing the same ole song—"My client is an entertainer, and those lyrics are just to entertain his fans. He's not really living the lifestyle he promotes." All of this is to say that when entertainers or athletes have a heavy influence over a swath of people, they inherently become role models. By choice or not, it just comes with the territory, and there's a big responsibility to bear when wielding such influence over the masses.

Men have long dominated hip-hop, but what about the women? Dating back to the late '80s, women like Roxanne Shanté, MC Lyte, and a host of others have had a huge influence on women in our culture. In '95, Queen Latifah received a Grammy for her song "Unity." This was in a time when rappers referred to women as bitches and hoes more increasingly. Latifah fearlessly challenged the notion of misogyny and male chauvinism by promoting love and self-respect. Thus, she raised the consciousness of women all over the world and became a role model to many fatherless daughters in the process.

Hip-hop was stronger than ever, and its kids were now becoming rich. Many of us from my generation had grown into young men who'd worked vigorously toward our monetary goals. In turn, many of us had created a path toward achieving financial stability for ourselves, and our families. But without a solid foundation of morals, ethics, and most importantly knowledge, a lot of those supposed material gains were nothing more than momentary. Without the proper information, capitalism can most certainly orchestrate your financial demise in a very startlingly short amount of time.

Around '99, while most people prepared for the new millennium, I was preparing for fatherhood. When my daughter Aiyanna was born, my very first thought was *Wow! She looks just like my mom!* I felt a love and a spiritual connection that I didn't previously know was possible. She would be raised in a world very different from the one that had raised me. I'd fought my way to a semi-comfortable position within Hollywood. I was still evolving as a young man, but I felt like the birth of my first child was my greatest accomplishment at that point. Nothing compared to the feeling of that spiritual connection to my child. I'd finally felt the pure love of a father, only it was emanating from my soul to hers. Before she was born, the relationship between her mother and I was on the verge of ending. So I knew she wouldn't grow up to see her parents together in that way, but I also knew I'd be there every single step of the way. Nothing and no one could stop that, point-blank, period!

Though I'd been in a couple of relationships prior, the relationship with my daughter's mother was basically the first lifelong bond I'd ever created with a woman outside of my family. When I was a kid, I didn't understand how two people could separate after creating a life together. Once more, hindsight is twenty-twenty. The failed relationship with my daughter's mother gave me some firsthand experience on the matter. At age twenty-six, I still hadn't really forgiven my father for his absence in my life, but I could no longer blame him for the demise of his and my mother's relationship. I learned that no child could keep a family together if it's just not meant to be. That realization brought about new questions that I was then old enough to understand. I absolutely adored my daughter, and I'd never intended on raising her in a broken home, so to say, but life can be very unpredictable at times.

As a kid, my life was based around structure, from my mom's rules in the household, to learning the right way to read a defense when I played for the Brooklyn Skyhawks, to following the extremely time-sensitive scheduling of a film shoot. This structure carried through to my adult life professionally, where I had everything worked out down to the details. But for me, there was no structure to being a father. It was the only role I wasn't properly prepared for. So in the beginning I was discombobulated. There's no manual or instruction booklet for parenthood. I mean, sure, there are plenty of books you can read on how to prepare, but none of them can truly prepare you for the real-world experiences. You can also get plenty of advice from whomever, but no one ever tells you just how scary parenthood can be. From throughout the pregnancy to the birth, there is an enormous amount of fear that can gnaw at you when you become a parent. Before my daughter, my thoughts were mostly centered around the next project, the next investment, the next fling, and so on.

But after she was born, I'd think about the increasing pollution of the world, climate change, her college tuition, and such. My daughter gave me an ability to see further into the future.

Financially, I could handle the responsibilities of parenthood, because my time was spent securing our lives in that way, but whenever fatherhood called, what was I supposed to do? I couldn't tell some director to stop filming because my daughter needed to be fed. Of course she'd be with her mom during those times, but to rely on her mom in that way felt a bit weak to me. Both parents should shoulder the responsibilities of their children. Fortunately, Aiyanna's mother understood, to a degree, the business I was in. But I refused to allow Hollywood to disrupt those bonding moments that were meant for my daughter and I.

I would learn pretty quickly that children don't fit into any schedule; they alter it. For the most part, toddlers require plenty of attention, food, patience, and an occasional diaper change. Spending alone time with my daughter when she was two years old was as much for me as it was for her. Of course the love I have for her will never waver, but the bond I was building with her was determined solely by the time we spent together. Witnessing her first steps and hearing her mumble "Da-Da" gave me an immense joy. No matter how hard my workday was, her smile and bright eyes lit up my heart. To everyone else, I was some celebrity, but to my daughter, I was her superman. Since I'd come into the business, I'd had to move in rooms full of vultures that only saw me as a commodity. Before I really knew who I was as a human being, I had to decipher who truly cared about me as a person in general and not my status. My daughter was a reaffirmation of sorts that I was worthy. Funny though, I'd often wonder about when I was a baby—had my father stuck around long enough to hear me attempt to say "Da-Da"?

Sometimes, in order to channel certain emotions for a character, all I had to do was think about never seeing my daughter or her beautiful smile again. So not only was she teaching me how to be a better man, but indirectly, she had a hand in me becoming a better artist. And yeah, I knew my career in Hollywood would eventually have an impact on our time together. Sometimes, I would have to choose. I couldn't put all I'd worked for on hold to be a full-time father in that regard. But that's what her mom was there for, right? Not exactly. The cure is balance. A child needs both mother and father. Still, nothing—and I mean nothing in this world—can compare to the bond between a mother and her child. From the inception, a mother carries her child within her own body. How does a man emotionally tap into that same type of connection with his kids while also still being the provider? Well, as they say, teamwork makes the dream work, and coparenting effectively definitely takes a lot of teamwork.

It seems like the world has stripped men down to being a toolbox, a pair of dirty work boots, and a pickup truck. Most men's true meaning has become equated to their bank accounts. In my opinion, that causes most men to develop chauvinistic ideals. Whether he works at FedEx, is a teacher, or is the head of a Fortune 500 company, being a provider becomes a man's lifelong mission, and his children can become footnotes to the book on his pursuit for success. How many stories have we heard of wealthy fathers who give their kids whatever their hearts desire, only for those kids to somehow still manage to get into pools of hot water? Some say kids who're spoon-fed a lavish lifestyle quickly become jaded and lack common sense because of the financial safety blankets their fathers provide. How can any kid respect rules and order if his or her father can simply write a check to make every problem go away? Now, did I spoil my daughter? Absolutely. But there must be balance. As they say, *everything in moderation*. Too many fathers throw money at their kids' mental and emotional issues, and eventually that only leads to much greater problems.

CHAPTER 4
California Flow

Please send me a pops before puberty,
the things I wouldn't do to see a piece of family unity.
—Tupac Shakur, "Papa'z Song"

An infant being born is literally a living miracle, and the bond between mother and child begins in the womb. If we men had to endure the mental, emotional, and physical experience of childbearing, we'd understand the true sacrifice it takes to actually carry a life in one's own body. A man's role in the process of creating a life only takes seconds, whereas a woman's entire world changes dramatically for nine months. Within that same time frame, a man can physically spread his seed to as many women as he chooses. I believe for some men, that dynamic gives them the false illusion of a godly power of sorts, in that if there was one man left on earth with ten women, humanity would survive. But if the tables were turned, our species would most likely become extinct.

Aiyanna's mother and I coparented the best we could, but I'd often think about the psychological impact our situation would have on Aiyanna. Would she one day blame me the same way I'd blamed my father, for her mother and I not being together? I tried not to miss all those precious, once-in-a-lifetime moments, but my career would cause me to miss a few of them. In those moments, my thoughts defaulted to it being my duty to provide. Regardless of the reality that my relationship with her mom was over, I had to be two steps ahead of any latent psychological effects I felt Aiyanna would encounter moving forward.

A sizable percentage of the parents in this nation are divorced and or single parents. And at that time, so was I. My mom had done it all by herself, so I didn't feel anything abnormal in that regard. Life goes on, and we've got to keep pushing. As fathers in particular, though, I believe we've become too accustomed to child support checks and weekend visits. There are other solutions. In some cases maybe not, but imagine a world in which breaking up the family unit was frowned upon instead of accepted.

I'd dedicated my life to not being anything like my father, but was I in some way repeating the same pattern? I mean, my daughter would never be fatherless, but she would grow up in a broken home just like I did. I felt like I was a good father, but that was by my standards. What about my daughter's standards? She would never have memories of her mom and dad living together in the same household. If I'd grown up with both of my parents in the household, would I have fought harder to keep my relationship with Aiyanna's mom intact? Instead of being guided through the situation by knowledge I could've only gotten from an older, wiser man who'd been through it already, I learned from experience. Which is often the hard way. And another cohesive black family unit ceased to exist in a traditional way.

Now, in an idealistic world, fathers are husbands. A man and woman make a conscious decision to solidify their union by creating a life together, thus becoming a family unit. But at that point in my life, the situation was what it was. Marriage? I definitely wasn't ready for all of that yet. In fact, at the time, I didn't think I'd ever get married. When it came to my love life, I was enjoying myself, spending many frivolous nights surrounded by the noise, but also kind of feeling alone.

My main focus was to be the best father I could be and, in the process, hopefully break the cycle of fatherlessness in my family for generations to come. My daughter was my new purpose and direction. Up until her birth, proving my father wrong had been a sizable part of my motivation deep in the recesses of my mind. However, as I'd sit alone in my plush bachelor pad surrounded by material baubles, I'd wonder if I'd somehow gone astray. Had I become too comfortable with being a co-parent? Did my daughter feel my absence when I wasn't around? She was too young to have a conversation about why I wasn't home to kiss her and tell her bedtime stories every night, but that didn't mean those thoughts didn't exist for her. Like the old saying goes, "If a tree falls in the forest and no one is around to hear it, does it make a sound?" To me, yes, that tree makes a sound, because logic will always trump opinions. Metaphorically, a fatherless kid is like that falling tree. You might not be able to hear or see a child's pain, but it's still there.

At times, it seemed as if some of the roles I played on film were almost parallel to my real life. Around that time, I did a movie called *The Wood*, which tells a story about childhood friends who help to teach each other how to become men. That is a similar depiction of my friendships with Marlon, G, Jeff, and Mitch. The character I played, Mike, is nothing like Q from *Juice*, but they have one thing in common; they're fatherless. I was still a novice at fatherhood by that point, but still, it started to dawn on me to question why those characters didn't have fathers. Though they were just characters to me, I began to wonder, what were the life experiences of the writers of those characters that they were synonymous in that specific way? Over the years, I've learned to separate myself from the characters I play on-screen. That method of discipline has kept me sane in real life, but such ironies of similarity would still pique my curiosity away from those movie sets. All the characters I've played were challenged by a whole different set of thoughts and emotions, which in turn caused me to be challenged by new notions of my own.

At that point, I'd already moved to Los Angeles to be in the epicenter of the entertainment business. I'd come a long ways from the concrete jungle called New York. Hollywood had a majestic feel to it, and it was the perfect atmosphere for a single man. That move would open up many professional doors but also cause other personal ones to close. The first to close slightly was my communication with my family back on the east coast. Still, I was always reachable. In LA, I was living in a different time zone, I was constantly on the go, and I was still learning how to be a parent. My family understood to a degree, but I could feel that they expected more from me. I'd anonymously handle certain things for them here and there, but my time is what they really needed. And as it's said, time is the most invaluable commodity in life. Surely, you live and you learn, and I tried my best. But my life at that point was moving at a completely different speed. Plus, there's no manual that comes with success. It's all trial and error. I guess it's as they say—heavy is the head that wears the crown.

In my younger days, when my boys and I talked about making it big, we never imagined the toll it would take on our families. I mean I was doing exactly what I was supposed to be doing—grabbing the bull by the horns and proactively putting in the work to fulfill my purpose. But back then I didn't know how to balance my time accordingly. And so I sort of became a picture on my family's wall. I was a single dad, and the two most important things in my life were moving at completely different speeds. While my daughter was learning her ABC's, my career was dashing toward a never-ending finish line. I definitely needed to find the balance. Though, I'd quickly learn that achieving what I'd accomplished in that time period was just the beginning. Marathon, not sprint; remember? But I was still growing as a man, with no guidance on how to juggle fatherhood and career, so I guess I was deficient in some ways.

I'd think about my mother a lot, and the number one question that riddled my mind was, *How did she do it?* For some reason, a lot of women have this keen ability to balance themselves in life like trapeze artists. I'd watch her day in and day out pursue her goals, sometimes working 12-14 hour days in the NYC public schools as a teacher, assistant principal, principal, and deputy superintendent. All the while raising me with no assistance, financial or otherwise. It's nothing short of amazing. So the question would burn in my mind: *How did she do it?* And she did it with way less money, fewer resources, and less access. So why the hell was I struggling to find that balance?

It's almost impossible to tell any man he isn't a great father when his kid is financially secure, especially one who grew up fatherless himself.

That's where the "I'm here, ain't I?" at the beginning of this book spawned from. It's obviously essential that every kid's needs are met financially, but sadly, in a lot of cases with broken homes, once a dollar amount is agreed upon, the father's involvement with the child withers away. If all a man contributes to his child is money, he's then devalued that child's life. Most fathers take pride in how they provide for their children, but we also must take pride in how we nurture our kids. That's not the role of mothers alone. Some men have diminished their own parental roles to just cutting a check. Cutting a check without providing the mental and emotional stability children need creates kids who won't understand the full importance of the bond between themselves and their fathers. It can also create parents who won't understand the same, because that's part of the cycle.

So I was being pulled in multiple directions and sometimes didn't know which way to turn. Was it possible to be everywhere at all times? My daughter, my mom, my sister, my family, and my friends each looked at me differently, but they all had similar expectations. I'd earned the position as head of the family. But without a blueprint or manual to give me insight, I had to find my own way.

Los Angeles nightlife was much different from New York's. Clear skies and sunny weather were more than enough to keep a single man's heart content and distracted. At age twenty-eight, I understood my responsibilities as a father, and emotionally, I'd learned how to compartmentalize things and focus on the moment. Was it selfish of me to not stay in an unproductive relationship with Aiyanna's mother for the sake of our daughter? What about my own happiness? Preservation of self is a paramount rule of life. Plus, all I was doing was pursuing my dreams and fulfilling my purpose on this here earth. My career had taken me from a small two-bedroom apartment in Brooklyn to the big, bright, blinding lights of Hollywood. But my daughter had me constantly evaluating self. No one else had that ability, but at a mere two years old, she did. I could be with any woman I wanted, but continually having meaningless trysts with women I had no interest in, other than physically, eventually got boring. *Am I the kind of guy I would want my daughter to date?* I'd wonder. Today I would say yes. But back then, I'm really not sure.

There was this one woman I'd known since I was eighteen, and though we'd briefly dated in the past, we also had an uncanny, genuine friendship. From time to time, I'd always wonder what would've become of us had we gotten serious in the past. Interestingly enough, it was me who'd suggested we not date back in the day and instead focus on our friendship. I just always felt an authentic, unique connection with her, and I was more scared of losing that than I was of taking the easy road with her.

Her name is Keisha. To me, she was much more than the lead singer of the legendary R&B group Total. She was a total enigma. Stunningly beautiful, extremely creative and feisty, her energy was something I'd never experienced. The universe knew that bringing me a life partner would give me the completeness that I needed, even though I myself was unaware of the need at the time. Plus, she herself was in the entertainment industry, so she fully understood the sometimes manic ways of an artistic soul. She'd touched my heart in ways that I'll never be able to put into words. And once again, God's divine poetry wrote itself into the book of my life when Keisha and I reconnected as adults.

Now, Keisha didn't have any children. In fact, she'd never in her life been pregnant. Obviously Aiyanna's mom could never be replaced, but Keisha was someone who was extremely loving and naturally maternal. It takes a very special kind of woman to love a child she didn't bear herself. I knew Keisha was full of love and light, but did she possess that super, special love needed for my daughter? Did she possess the patience and ability to compromise and sacrifice in order to deal with my daughter's mother? Honestly, I knew she had all those qualities, and more, in her heart.

I'd purposefully never brought another woman around my daughter, so when Aiyanna and Keisha first met, the feeling was pure. The doorbell rang, and I picked my daughter up, kissed her on the cheek, and told her, "There's someone I'd like you to meet." Aiyanna simply stared at me with innocent eyes. She had no idea her father had now found the love of his life and was awaiting her approval. Holding her closely in my arms, I walked to the door, took a deep breath, and opened it. Keisha stood in the doorway with a warm smile on her face, and without hesitation she reached for my daughter. I was mesmerized by Keisha's spirit. She instantly fell in love with Aiyanna, and I fell deeper in love with her in that very moment. There's no one way to raise a child, but one thing's for sure: it really does take a village. And now, my daughter had more than just her biological parents loving her; she also had the unconditional love of the woman I was in love with.

At some point, men have to grow out of the mind-set of planting seeds without tending to the garden. Don't get me wrong—it's not easy to find the person you want to spend the rest of your life with, but if you choose to be a single parent versus choosing to build a family with someone, you're selling your offspring short. A kid deserves both parents, and breaking the cycle of fatherlessness begins with you. Too many men run the streets putting jezebels on a pedestal instead of glorifying women who are wifey material. If Keisha hadn't come into my life, I would've had to deal with the limited role of being a single parent. After all, that's the norm of today and days past, right? In most cases, any family court will make the mother the custodial parent instead of implementing equal rights for both parents. Too many fathers are content with just having weekends with their kids. Is that because they've fulfilled their financial obligations and thus coach themselves to believe their job has been done? Too many fathers don't fight in the initial stages of determining custodial and visitation rights. And when those relationships go sour, it's then an uphill legal battle to become an active father.

Since I was a solid provider before Keisha, I didn't feel the need to prove to anyone other than my daughter that I was a good father. It was also important, though, that Keisha knew there was much more to me in that regard. And she, in turn, was much more than a shoulder to lean on. She gave my daughter the same kindheartedness that my mother had given to me as a child. I enjoyed watching them bond together, and I found more time to make those moments possible. I began to slowly figure out how to find the balance between family and career. It's not at all easy to deprogram oneself from the deep-rooted messages about parenthood that we've been indoctrinated with when you come from where we come from, but it's absolutely necessary to do so. And trying something new is the first step to freeing one's mind from the shackles of past mistakes. Before Keisha, I was just a man and a father. But after her, I became the patriarch of my family.

During those early stages, my daughter's mom gave me the space I needed to selfishly drive my career. For sure, though, she'd question why she was only good enough to be my baby's mama and not my girlfriend or wife. That was similar to the confusion I felt when I first met my sister. I didn't actually understand how my father could've created a new life before he'd even invested into mine. I wished I had the words to ease Aiyanna's mom's insecurities and disappointment, but I knew Keisha and I were destined to be. Many men have chosen to stay in a relationship for the sake of the children, and I empathize with those who've sacrificed their own happiness for perception. But what's real is real, and what is a family truly if it's only a family on the surface for the look? I knew Aiyanna's mother loved me, and I loved her. Just not in the same way. The reality is I loved her like a sister. Not in some weird type of way, but when it came down to the brass tacks of our connection, that's just what I'd felt with her from the very first day that we met. A spiritual, sibling kind of love. I was the product of a broken home, and so was she. So neither one of us ever wanted that for our daughter, but alas, God had other plans. I knew that truth would be a very hard pill for her to swallow.

The more time Keisha spent with my daughter, the more their relationship blossomed. Keisha willingly accepted the role of bonus mom. Even though Aiyanna was still a toddler, the clock was ticking for me to have "that" conversation with her mother, especially because another woman was now spending time with our daughter. I wanted her mom to be happy and respect that I'd found someone who would care for our daughter with love and compassion. I didn't know how she'd respond, though. Up until that point, we had a mutual agreement on my financial obligations and the like, but now, I had to wrap my mind around the possibility of going through family court.

I understood the purpose of child support, but something about utilizing a heartless, sometimes unjust system to settle the matters of child custody didn't sit well with me. I knew the conversation with Aiyanna's mother would be difficult, but I also had faith that we were mature enough to do what was best for our daughter. The child support system in America isn't supposed to be a big bad wolf that rips families apart, but unfortunately, that's exactly what it is, and that's exactly what it does. The system is used as a means to control and manipulate. In my opinion, ego and pride are why so many parents place the fate of their children into the hands of a cold and ruthless family court system. A kid becomes a docket number, and a person whom you've never met before will determine what is best for your child. I didn't feel comfortable with giving some stranger, cloaked in a robe, holding a gavel, that type of power over what's ultimately my responsibility. And neither should any man.

During this time, my spirituality grew immensely. I'd pray for many things, but the words I then uttered to God, regarding the situation hanging over my head, required me to bare all. I was completely vulnerable. And that's right where the Most High wanted me. My conversations with God were sometimes fulfilling, and other nights, there was complete silence.

During those moments of silence, I felt remorse for the disappointment Aiyanna's mother would endure. She'd have to deal with the embarrassment of not being chosen. With the rest of the world, she would witness two public figures proclaiming their love for one another, a love she felt she deserved. Magazines and radio stations would glamorize my relationship with Keisha like a fairy tale, and the public's opinion and scrutiny would spread like a wildfire. And yet all I was doing was following my heart. Simplicity. Even though my daughter was only three years old at the time, I was also concerned about her perception of it all. How would she feel when she saw her father's relationship with another woman on the cover of a magazine or blog? I had to prepare myself for every scenario, and it was imperative that I handled those situations delicately.

Keisha always found ways to soothe my anxiety. She understood my perspective and gave me the confidence I needed to address the situations.

She understood how important it was to make the coparenting situation work, not only for me, but also for us as a team. She was a great mother to Aiyanna. She knew her role and respected the boundaries. I knew I would one day make Keisha a mother, by blood, herself. And I also knew that our unborn children would never have to find one another the same way I had to find my sister in days past. To this day, I still don't understand how my father could create other lives and leave it up to his children to connect the dots. Everything I've accomplished up to this point would mean nothing if my children had to grow up apart. It's easy to look away and let the chips fall where they may, but ultimately, that only leads down a path of confusion and pain for any kid. Life is a balancing act. And for me, falling off of the tightrope was just never an option.

While I was mentally preparing to take my next steps forward, my sister, Aisha, was becoming a woman right under my nose. My relationship with her was then only seven years old, but our bond had already bloomed into solid sibling flow. Unlike our father, I'd been dedicated to earning her trust. She was nineteen then, so by law, she was a young adult. But to me, she was still that shy little twelve-year-old girl whom our father had abandoned. One day, I received a call from her, and her silence was a clear sign that something was bothering her. She mumbled, "I'm pregnant." My jaw dropped. *WTF! How could this be? Where did I go wrong? Hold up, I'm an uncle now? Who's the father, and why haven't I met him?* Even though she was a young adult who could make her own choices, I struggled with how to respond. The bottom line was I loved my sister. So, though I was a bit disappointed in her for becoming pregnant at such a young age, we'd adapt accordingly and persevere. Patriarch shit.

When I was nineteen, I was growing up and in the entertainment business. The way my sister was growing up at that age would now be much more difficult. There would be no glitz, glamour, money, or fame. Instead, she would face the realities of motherhood. Needless to say, the news of her pregnancy was a hard pill for me to swallow, but I could feel her waiting for my blessing. She expected me to scold her harshly, and she was absolutely terrified. I know this because we've discussed that moment after the fact. I thought about my mom and how she would've responded had I come home with that news at nineteen. Those weren't pretty thoughts in any shape, fashion, or form.

As I stood holding the phone in silence, I thought about the struggle she would face. I assumed her situation would be similar to most single mothers with little to no support from the father. The thought of her dealing with all of that alone was frightening to me. So, before I finally responded, I gathered myself. I was her big brother and father figure. And I knew she needed to feel supported, not shamed. Again, marathon over sprint.

She told me she was six months pregnant. Wow! What disturbed me more than the news of her pregnancy was finding out so late. That was the moment I realized she really saw me more as a father figure than a brother. And that was a bit overwhelming. The reason she didn't tell me earlier was simply because of fear. There's that damn word again, *fear* … Fear is poison to our spirits. But back to the story. Six whole months? I mean we'd had vague conversations about her dealings with guys, but *motherhood*? I'd never seen that coming so soon for her. Yeah, I lived in a different time zone, and yes, I was constantly on the go, but how the hell did I miss that one?

They say, "To whom much is given, much is expected." My sister never gave me the impression that she didn't take heed of my advice, but advice without authoritative reinforcement is just words. We all have different processes. For some, all it takes is a conversation; others require much more than that to get the message and learn the lesson. Regardless of the situation, my niece would be taken care of. I'd see to that. I'd prepare Aisha as best I could for the perils of parenthood and make sure she would become the best mother she could be.

I couldn't hide from my father's mistakes. I knew what type of cloth he was cut from, but I'm sure deep down my sister hoped that becoming a grandfather would make him take on the responsibility he'd been avoiding. She was wrong. See, he'd been out of my life completely, but for her, he was sometimes in, though mostly out. I never wanted to rain on her parade when it came to her expectations of our father. I knew she had to form her own opinions.

Three months later, my niece was born, and our father would treat his grandchild the same way he'd treated us. In my eyes, he'd found a comfort in whatever excuses or rationalizations he had in his mind when it came to his absence in our lives. And now, those things extended to his granddaughter. Most people who become parents wish to live long enough to become grandparents, and here my father was throwing that away. So? I decided to fortify Aisha's mind and soul with clarity. *This isn't your cross to bear. It's his and his alone. You've done nothing wrong, so don't even for a moment burden yourself with the weight of that man's actions.* There she was newly minted in motherhood yet still dealing with the repercussions of our father's absence. Either way, moving forward, he would live in that pit of misery all by himself.

My sister and I have had many conversations about our father, and I took more time to try to decipher his shortcomings after my niece was born. Even though he continued his pattern of absence, it wasn't easy for Aisha to detach from our father. My sister has memories of them briefly spending time together at the playground when she was little; I don't. It's like even that small gesture, from him to her, was enough to plant a false seed of hope. Regardless of his bleak parental résumé, she was a daughter who still wanted her father. Who was I to criticize her for feeling something that's universally natural? According to the teachings of all religions, ultimately, forgiveness is mandatory. Forgiveness should flow out of our hearts like a river to a waterfall, but I think at times even God knows that's certainly not an easy task.

Through my daughter, I experienced what a father-daughter bond should feel like, so I knew what my sister was missing in that regard. Thus, my own fatherhood sort of created a new level of disdain, on my end, for our father's absence in her life. I was in constant prayer when it came to her, and I found myself at an impasse within my heart. I needed God to soften me, so I wouldn't interfere with Aisha's potential of kindling a relationship with our father. I came to the conclusion that if he wanted to die a lonely man, so be it, but if having an active relationship with his daughter was still in his heart, then I'd have to adjust. Back when I was a kid, I knew what it felt like to think about my father on a daily basis, hoping for change. I never wanted Aisha to feel that kind of disappointment, but it was too late. The birth of my niece reopened my sister's wound of fatherlessness.

Growing up fatherless is one thing, but becoming a fatherless parent comes with an entirely different set of feelings in one's heart and thoughts in one's mind. When it came to the trail of disappointment our father fostered in our hearts, I knew the questions that would keep my sister up at night. At times, I worried for her more than she'll ever know. It's a great feeling to witness the joy and completeness a grandchild brings to his or her grandparents, and she was robbed of that joy when it came to our father. It was imperative that I proved my niece was loved and protected, regardless of his absence. Aisha was tough, and she shielded her emotions from the world, but beyond her wall of defense, I saw a daughter who desired logical answers— a woman who deserved answers. It amazed me how this man, my father and hers, was the source of so much pain and dis-content within us. Surely, forgiving a man like him would take a miracle.

CHAPTER 5

Queen Meets King

To support mother and father, to cherish wife and children—
this is the greatest blessing.

—Buddha

The thought of marrying Keisha was always present. She was my completion, and we were inseparable. Instead of working strenuous hours and then coming home to her, I kept Keisha by my side at all times. My love life was no longer something I dealt with only when the time permitted; instead, Keisha had access to my entire world. Any relationship will always reach points of frustration or what have you, but any couple that truly enjoys each other's presence will learn that communication is essential. She and I enjoyed, and still do enjoy, each other's company. Relationships will be what they are. Some are good; others are toxic. But for me, finally being in a healthy relationship was teaching me a lot. And though my mind-set was refreshed and renewed, it was all uncharted terrain.

Many co-parents are faced with the same scenario, and in a lot of cases, a whole lot of drama tags along. It's not easy for a woman to share her title of "mother." Some parents discipline their children harshly for calling another person Mom or Dad. In my opinion, that approach is selfish and has an instant negative effect on the child. Some people even use that tactic as a means to control. In too many cases, a man who hasn't done his fair share of parental responsibilities will somehow find the time to speak up when his title is on the line. But where was that pride when his kid wanted him most? A father who builds a healthy relationship with his child will never have to fight for his title.

These kids are too young to understand that their fathers' shortcomings aren't a reflection of them but only a reflection of their fathers. Any parent who doesn't take pride in his or her own creation has an extremely low self-esteem. That low self-esteem is consequentially passed on to the child. Thus, before that child even knows who he or she is as a person, negativity has infiltrated his or her natural desire to strive for greatness.

As an adult, nothing should make you happier than knowing your child is comfortable in his or her own skin. When a child is scolded for expressing love to a stepparent, it usually ends in that child forming resentment for the biological parent who has an issue. It takes a high level of maturity and an unselfish understanding to share your parental position with a person who isn't biologically connected to your kid. If you prefer your child to dislike his or her stepparent just because of your own issues, that says more about you than it does the stepparent. These types of selfish acts can lead to an identity crisis for some kids. If love is the vital ingredient to raising an emotionally stable child, parents should allow their children to receive as much love and guidance as they possibly can. Pride is the archenemy to such an ideology. Too often, when it comes to certain kinds of people, pride wins over love.

Now, as I said, Keisha had never been pregnant before in her entire life, so she was completely unfamiliar with the sensations and protocols that come with pregnancy. As a result, when she one day began having morning sickness among other things, she didn't identify that with having become pregnant. As I left for work that day, I told her to get a pregnancy test. When I returned home, she said it was positive, but she thought it was wrong. I asked if she'd gotten two pregnancy tests. She hadn't. I told her that was the normal course of action. Hey, what can I say? I was mostly raised around women, but to her, I'd only played a doctor on television. Well, she got a second test, and it too was positive. Wow! We were having a baby! We were so excited!

Keisha's excitement soon turned into disbelief. She called the hotline help number on the back of the pregnancy test and spoke to someone about the results. The representative told her that the test is 99 percent accurate and she should confirm with her doctor. She didn't believe the person and asked to speak to a supervisor, who told her the same thing. I was more than amused by her antics, but I was patient nonetheless, I understood that 1 percent chance of the test being wrong was more than enough of a possibility to drive her momentarily crazy. It wasn't until she had the sonogram and heard our child's heartbeat that all her skepticism disappeared. She instantly burst into tears. The pregnancy wasn't just a symbol of our love; it represented our forever. As far as I was concerned, I was having a kid with my future wife. We were family by blood now, and I couldn't have chosen a better woman to create a life with, and a sibling for Aiyanna.

In that first trimester, as all parents know, all we wanted was a healthy child. As Keisha's stomach grew, so did my daughter's curiosity. I would constantly say, "You're going to be a big sister." She was in love with the idea. Aiyanna wasn't your typical four-year-old; she was keenly observant, and I could see her mind putting the pieces together. Whenever Keisha wobbled around, Aiyanna would press her face against Keisha's belly. Life is so beyond interesting. I didn't know my sister until I was twelve years old, and here my daughter was showing compassion and love for her sibling who was still in the womb. That made me extremely proud as a father.

K'mari was born, and I was there every step of the way. When my first daughter was born, I vowed to forever love and protect her. And when my second daughter was born, I made the same exact vow to God and the universe. As I held K'mari in my arms, the reality of her being yet another living miracle hit me like a bolt of lightning.

Women literally risk their lives when they're in the process of giving birth, and the weight of that wasn't lost on me when it came to Keisha. Overall, I experienced a very different feeling mentally though. I'd morphed from having a single father's mentality to having a family man's mentality. See, I can relate to any man who isn't in love with the woman he's creating a life with. Though I loved Aiyanna's mother, that part of our relationship had long passed, and I wasn't *in love* with her when Aiyanna was born. The opposite stood in my heart when it came to Keisha. We were very much in love when our first child was born. So how could I not want to make her an "honest woman"?

Traditionally, a man and woman would tie the knot before having a kid, but a lot of times it is what it is. It's funny how men are so apprehensive when it comes to marriage, but they don't exhibit the same caution when it comes to getting a woman pregnant. Marriage is a contract in a legal sense, and in a spiritual sense. Married or not, it's all about having a healthy relationship with the one you love, because that can help you be better parents if you two have kids. Toxic relationships lead to negative circumstances, which have damaging impacts on a child's psyche. In those instances, kids can become like side effects of an unhealthy situation. So, for me, K'mari's birth was also a symbolic graduation from the failures associated with a broken relationship.

Something about being a big sister resonated with Aiyanna in ways I can't explain. She was an only child growing up in a coparenting environment, but the birth of her little sister changed that reality. I'd dread when Aiyanna had to leave because I would see the disappointment on her face—not because she didn't want to be with her mother but because she simply wanted to spend more time with her sister. All the money in the world couldn't change what she felt when she was detached from her sister. So I took the time to explain to her the dynamics of our family. Though she was still too young to truly comprehend the situation, I led with my heart and told her to do the same. As coparents, her mom and I decided to split her time evenly. That way her schedule operated like a well-oiled machine. Personally, I'd never experienced the effects of growing up in two different households. Though Aiyanna had to adjust to different rule sets and the like, she received the same love equally from both households.

Everything for me as a father was now doubled. As had happened so many times before in my life, a voice in my head whispered, *You'd better get*

your ass to work! I'd be wiser this go-round, though
whenever that voice whispered in my mind, I'd ins
nonstop. But that mind-set was what had caused
those once-in-a-lifetime moments early on with Aiya
"Family first" became my new mantra. They say you
Well, at that point I was doing both simultaneously.

The stars were really aligning for me personally and
and it felt like the perfect time to marry the love of my life.
the left of the pastor awaiting my beautiful bride to walk dow
glanced at my mother, then an ordained Deacon in the African
Episcopal Church, as she prepared to co-officiate the ceremony
at my soon-to-be mother-in-law. Then my two daughters, who w
flower girls, started down the aisle, sprinkling rose petals. I felt
of completion. We'd chosen to have a bare-bones wedding cerem
pomp and circumstance—mainly because my rigorous work sch
made it nearly impossible to plan and execute a big wedding with al
bells and whistles, but also because of what that moment truly mean
us and to us alone. Our wedding ceremony was not only a proclamati
of the union of two souls but also a divine victory. I was showing m
daughters the authentic essence of a man at the highest level through an
ordained celebration of the power of love. The doors swung open, and
there she was, my life's commitment for better or worse. One of my favorite women in the universe was walking down the aisle to me. That was
the moment I forever changed the perception of the men in my bloodline.

Husband. The word alone gives a man his entry into a league of extraordinary gentlemen. Only a few really embrace such a sacrifice. Ideally,
becoming a husband is saying no to the flesh and yes to the spiritual realm
of a relationship. I didn't need the ceremony to know that my connection
to Keisha was spiritual, but it felt damn good to show my commitment
publically. There's no rulebook to fatherhood, and there damn sure isn't
one to becoming a husband, but I'd committed to trying my best.

Some fatherless men who then become husbands struggle with such
a transition. Others compile all the experiences they learned from dating

ll the dice, hoping it works in a marriage. How many young boys
witnessed their parents engage in a disagreement, then reconcile and
empathy toward one another? How many young girls have smiled
eir fathers' passion for their mothers? How many children have heard
r parents say "I love you" to one another? Broken family structures
countless children of having those learning experiences, and every-
carries the baggage from their upbringings into their adulthood.

Instead of having the tools needed to help foster healthy unions of
heir own, many people are tasked with mending together the shards of
he failed relationships they grew up around and imbue all of that into
their own relationships once they come of age. On the outside, many
of us who come from broken families may appear normal, but beneath
those facades, a lot of us wallow in self-doubt and, in the most extreme
cases, self-hate. People go on wishing that new romantic endeavors can
mend those years of concealed pain, but those roads often lead to even
more disappointment. People want to vent and express themselves openly
to those they love without judgment. I believe all healthy relationships
begin with understanding—understanding of the other's individual life
journey and all he or she has gone through to get where he or she is. In
every example on record, you'll find those answers hidden in the depths
of a person's childhood experiences.

I opened up to Keisha about my own childhood, and in doing so, she
got a deep insight into the mental and emotional road I'd traveled from
then to the present. Bringing her into my creative world was cool, but
allowing her into those vulnerable spaces I'd closed off in my heart is
really what helped us build an unbreakable bond. She'd also grown up
in a fractured relationship with her father, and having that in common
gave us an ability to see each other's shortcomings in a different light.
We understood one another in a kinetic sense. Our hearts spoke in a
language that didn't require us to always speak with our mouths. And
that was simply because we both allowed each other into our sheltered
places of innocence and heartbreak. We accepted each other's imperfections. As a matter of fact, we saw our imperfections as perfections in their
own ways. Knowing that the first man to ever really disappoint my wife

was her father helped me to understand her better when she had certain moments of insecurity or what have you. See, if we hadn't taken the time to find out from whence we'd come individually, our union would've lacked the foundation needed to overcome matters of the heart and trust moving forward.

In the natural flow of the universe, it's difficult for any woman to fully comprehend the role of being a mother or wife if she's never received the proper definition or guidance before, and the same goes for any man in terms of being a father or husband. At the highest level of consciousness, a man understands he is the Alpha and Omega within his household. That position isn't at all to be given; it's only to be earned. You aren't a lion simply because you have a mane and long teeth. You must endure the battles and earn the scars to truly hold such a prestigious title.

I was fortunate in that I had two daughters who naturally gravitated toward the femininity that Keisha provided. Playing with dollhouses, having tea parties, playing dress-up, and mimicking Beyoncé's choreography was their lane organically. Our home was healthy, and my girls were happy.

The older my daughters became, though, the more I started to see a clear difference in the dynamics of having a single two-parent home versus two separate homes. K'mari experienced a certain consistency, and she was a part of the new generation in my family to witness her parents live in the same household, in real time. I'd taken pride in being the first to break that cycle, and she was the living product of that structural transition. Beyond her own personality, K'mari possessed a certain calmness, because her reality was simple. Meanwhile, at nine years old, Aiyanna was being pulled into two different directions mentally. We did everything we could to let her know she could never be two people in one body, but I couldn't control her personal need to feel it out for herself. Ultimately, I knew she had to find her own way of balancing all of that within her own heart and mind. It bothered me not knowing what type of child my daughter was like when she wasn't in our care. I'm sure she was well taken care of, but as her father, it was natural for me to want to know those types of things. I was totally comfortable with how my wife filled the void on her end. She had the ability to peel back more layers than I could at times, so I took it upon myself to help facilitate moments for only Keisha and Aiyanna to share. In a sense, that put me on a tightrope, because I was trying to balance my time with both my daughters' hearts and their different personalities. I never wanted the moments I facilitated for Aiyanna to cause K'mari to feel alienated, and vice versa.

As parents, sometimes we feel the need to explain ourselves to our kids, in an attempt to be better understood by them. And that's okay, but in all honesty, when your intent is pure, just let God work. K'mari was still very young and not as vocal as Aiyanna, but she dealt with our blended family dynamic a bit differently. I felt like I was the reason she couldn't bond with and enjoy her sister 24-7. Our conversations weren't yet as detailed as my conversations with Aiyanna, but I tried my best to explain the stipulations, if you will, of their sisterhood. To me, all of it further proved that even when coparenting responsibly is effective, sometimes the siblings on either side can suffer collateral damage in an emotional sense.

Sometimes when I spoke to Aiyanna over the phone, I could hear a difference in her tone. Whenever I questioned her about it, she'd brush it off as if it was nothing, but I knew she was suppressing whatever she truly felt in those moments. At that point, she was too advanced for the "Everything's going to be all right" mantra. I knew her thoughts were wrapped around the notion of "How's that going to play out?" But I also assumed she wasn't yet ready for a conversation about why her mom and I didn't work out in that way.

Too often, parents feel the need to put on a perfect persona for their children. Sharing the harsh truth with your kid, once he or she is ready of course, will give your kid a humanized perception of you. So, in an effort to keep an open line of communication between us, I gave it to Aiyanna straightforward. I shed my concerns and fears of how she'd interpret all that information. I just gave her the real, without any bias. The funny thing is, I knew she'd already seen and experienced exactly what the situation was. One thing is for sure: no matter how hard you try, no parent can ever really hide the truth from his or her kids, especially when they're around you day in and day out. They see it all! So, even though Aiyanna may have still been too young to cohesively put her feelings into words, when I gave her the real about her mom and me, she was already in the know emotionally. Thus, my efforts regarding that issue only brought us closer together.

CHAPTER 6

Watch the Throne

If the game shakes me or breaks me,

I hope it makes me a better man, take a better stand.

Put money in my mom's hand,

get my daughter this college grant,

so she don't need no man.

—Notorious B.I.G., "Sky's the Limit"

When Keisha and I found out we were once again pregnant, we just stared at each other nervously. Without uttering any words, we both knew what the other was thinking: *I hope it's a boy.* I believe every man naturally desires a son to carry on his name and legacy, and I was certainly no different. Keisha wanted a son as well, but as always, we just prayed for a healthy child. People really don't tell you just how scary pregnancy can be. So many things can go wrong; so many things can go awry, attributed to genetics, diet, environment, and more. Whether you believe in religion, or science, or both, it is astonishing when you stop and think about the trillions of events that literally need to happen in order to produce a human life into this world. At the end of the day, the birth of a baby is truly a mind-shattering miracle.

On the surface, I came off calm and ready, but deep down I was a nervous wreck. The first trimester always seems to take long, but this one felt like an eternity. And then ... we found out we were having a boy! I'd already kind of numbed my senses to the possibility of such, so much that

I ended up questioning the doctor. "Are you sure? I've heard about cases of mistaken genders." Ha! But the doctor was sure, as was my wife, and it was as if my life had come full circle in that moment. *Wow! The heir to my throne is in the womb!* I'd often stare at Keisha's stomach, envisioning my son and me doing the things that fathers and sons do. Though I'd finally get to experience the bond I'd never had as a child, the reality was a bit daunting. How would I be a father to my son without a blueprint on how to do so? It was a constant battle of the unknown that I couldn't escape. When all my children were born, they each represented a different benchmark, if you will, in my life. With the forthcoming birth of my son, *legacy* was what I felt in my soul.

Brooklyn's own would bring forth his young prince of the kingdom, one that I'd built from the ground up with blood, sweat, and tears. Keisha was now carrying one of the most integral pieces of my life's puzzle. As soon as his gender was confirmed, I instantly knew I didn't want to name him after me. I didn't want to rob him of his own identity in that sense. I could feel his spiritual energy too, so fittingly, I chose to name him Amir. And thus, I would be born again. Amir was the first great-grandson in my entire family, and they excitedly anticipated his arrival. He was the newest male branch on our family's tree that would continue to grow our bloodline for generations to come. My wife was illuminated with a very particular kind of glow; it was one of divine power.

I was extremely thankful God was giving me the opportunity to raise my own son into a man. And yes, I'd obviously had experience with being a father, but as any parent can attest, there's a world of difference between raising girls versus boys. As Keisha's stomach grew, I voraciously wondered if he would walk, talk, or act like me. When it came to the births of my daughters, I vividly remember being overwhelmed by the need to protect and provide. With my son, I felt more of a pressure to teach and be a living example.

I'd become a treasure chest of knowledge, and I'd finally have the opportunity to pass on all my years of wisdom, mistakes, victories, and failures to a son of my very own. He definitely wouldn't learn how to be a man from some rapper or athlete. No, he'd have a head start on manhood, simply by having his biological father in his life actively. He would have a working manual, a solid blueprint. Fortunately, he'd never have to learn the lessons that come from the ills of the hood like I did. But still, one day he'd know even those rules and be aware of them nonetheless.

My life's purpose began to evolve. Through an abyss of rampant thoughts and ideas about my son, I gained a deeper insight into who I was and what I stood for. He was the catalyst that propelled me to gain a stronger awareness of the universe's connectivity. Everything is alive, from the most minute microorganism to the earth itself. It's all alive, and we're all connected in some way. With thoughts like that carousing through my mind, I couldn't understand how any man wouldn't feel the burning desire to dedicate his life to guiding the life of his son. As fathers we all have the capability to mold our sons into someone greater than us. We often see that in sports, when the son exceeds the father—Floyd Mayweather Jr., Peyton and Eli Manning, Kobe Bryant, Steph Curry, and the list goes on. I've done well for myself, but nothing would please me more than to watch my son become greater than me in his life's pursuits. We should all want greatness for our kids, and one of the greatest rewards of fatherhood is having nurtured your children and witnessing them exceed your expectations.

At that point, for all my years of parenthood, I'd only known the mechanics of a father-daughter bond. Here, my son's due date was steadily approaching. One night it occurred to me that maybe, just maybe, my father had actually given me the greatest gift ever. As a child, I was extremely bitter about being fatherless, but all that pain came from not having a father-son relationship. So I'd never applied any of that baggage toward my daughters. Raising two girls somewhat shielded me from the lack of a father-son bond. Now that my prince was on the way, the things that I'd lacked as a son without his father would somehow teach me to father a son of my own. I'm speaking on the positives and negatives. As they say, do unto others as you would have them do unto you. Now, that revelation may not work for every guy, but if you too grew up fatherless, it can be a great start on finding out how to become a productive father yourself.

As guys, we all deserve our biological fathers' love, but we also shouldn't wallow in what we didn't receive as young boys in that regard. We should use those experiences to help guide us on the right path with our own sons. Don't get me wrong—there are some jagged bumps in the road when it comes to how a fatherless man raises his son. But nonetheless, we can become good fathers by raising our consciousness and fighting through those battles in our own minds.

Well, all the theories and speculations came to an end when my son was finally born. For nine months, I'd visualized the moment. When I pulled my prince into this world, I felt an overwhelming sense of completion. When my first child was born, I was ill prepared, in that I had nothing in my toolbox of fatherhood other than the power of love. When my second child was born, though still newly developed in fatherhood, at least I'd then had some real-world experiences. When my son was born, I was seasoned and ready—ready to raise my young prince into a king who will one day build a kingdom of his own.

He was merely a few weeks removed from his mother's womb, and I was steeped in fascination. I'd talk to him, and we'd stare at one another, speaking volumes in an unspoken language. My wife nurtured him the same way she nurtured our daughters, but there was a slight difference. She was completely smitten with him, and vice versa. To me, it has nothing to do with personalities and things of that nature; it's all about the laws of the universe. Man to woman, woman to man, father to daughter, mother to son. When he'd burst into a screeching cry and I'd try to console him, the simple sound of his mother's voice would immediately put him at ease. I never questioned the power of their connection, because I was a mama's boy myself. He knew his mother's energy, her touch, her scent, and it was like I was the one he had to get used to. So, in a way, I had to earn my own son's trust from when he was an infant, the same way I felt my father would've had to earn mine. The notion of such had never occurred to me before.

If a man isn't willing to wake up in the middle of the night to feed his own child or change a diaper, then he's not fulfilling the physical duties of fatherhood. As a father, you can't just love your kids from afar; you have to show your love through interacting with them. A lot of things about raising kids can feel like a game of luck or roulette, but in the end, this thing called fatherhood is meant to be done proactively, not in retrospect.

So who's to blame for the pandemic of fatherlessness that has stricken our communities for decades? Is it the school systems? Have they taken a lackluster approach to educating our youths about the consequences of having unprotected sex? Some would argue such topics should be dealt with in the home, and they're right. All education should begin in the home, but let's be honest—the real curiosity about sex begins at school among one's peers. Everything is way too politically correct nowadays. There are all these buffers and concerns of offending someone, so the brutal truth of things gets lost in the ether. Kids have developed a careless immaturity and thus an ability to emotionally detach from lifelong commitments. So, as a community at large, have we actually done this to ourselves? What has multiple generations of babies having babies, and mothers raising sons by themselves taught us? Let me sum it up to this: when it comes to boys, a mother's whisper will one day become faint, and if his father isn't there to reinforce that whisper, along with his own, the outcomes are usually disastrous.

My children would not only hear their mother's whisper; they'd also respect my reinforcement of it. The type of respect I'm referring to is not associated with the fear of any physical pain but rather the fear of disappointing me. My mom showed me that discipline through the fear of disappointment is real. As a kid, I didn't know what it felt like to hear my mom say, "I'm going to tell your father." She knew that threat would've been laughable to say the least. But those words should freeze any child where he or she stands and inspire a feeling of fearing an authority of law and order. Active fathers have the power to mold and guide their kids' paths to adulthood for the better.

Slowly but surely, my son grew from an infant into a toddler taking his first steps. I enjoyed holding him in my arms, but seeing him become mobile on his own two feet ignited a new spark in our bond. I would back up one step, extend my arms, and watch him stumble in my direction. One step turned into three. Three steps turned into me chasing him around the house soon after. I was aware that every day spent with him was me rewriting the history of fathers and sons within my family. He studied my every move, and I studied his as well. One particular night, I crept into his room while he was asleep and noticed we even slept the same exact way. There's no greater feeling than seeing hints of yourself within your own creation. As Genesis 1:27 (American Standard Version) says, "And God created man in his own image." The Bible contains many references to fatherhood for a reason. It's a supreme gift. It's a spiritual bond to eternity through one's own offspring, and it gives a sense of belonging that is incomparable to anything in this world.

CHAPTER 7
Reality Check

They say the coolest playas and foulest heart-breakers in the
world, God gets us back. He makes us have precious little girls.
—Nas, "Daughters"

Nowadays some parents allow their children to be exposed to sex,
drugs, and violence before they can even handle basic math. To
this day, I can still see that "line" when I'm in my mother's presence. That line is called respect. My mom didn't care to be the hip-
pest or speak in slang just to relate to me when I was younger. In our
neighborhood, mothers of days past truly represented wisdom and love.
They experienced a paradigm shift in society and lived through extreme
circumstances like the civil rights era. My mom strapped up her boots
and fought the difficult fight of raising me alone when the child support
system wasn't the safety blanket that it is now.

Eventually, a more sophisticated child support system was put into
place, which led to even more men being incarcerated. It's like there's
a war on everything *except* on fatherlessness! In a lot of cases with non-
payment of child support, once a man is released from jail, he can't find
employment. Then he resorts to other means to provide, which often
leads him down a path of recidivism. Now, many will argue that man put
himself in that position, and I agree, but how do we improve our legal
system to make room for the true redemption and rehabilitation of these
men? We've handed over our parental control to a system that isn't at all

concerned with the proper development of our children or our families. We really have to reanalyze who's actually benefitting from the child support system in this country.

Fatherhood in America is a complex issue, and yet it shouldn't be, though it's almost impossible to address it effectively without discussing race. Surely, the issue affects people of all races, but it's no secret that fatherlessness among black men has reached epidemic proportions. Whether it was J. Edgar Hoover railing against organized black leadership or Bull Connor railing against average, law-abiding black citizens, there's been, quite frankly, an aggressive war specifically on black men for centuries. Our great black leaders were killed, and thus their women and children were left abandoned. Of course times have changed drastically in that regard, but as the old saying goes, the more things change, the more they stay the same. It's 2018 now, and those white supremacist ways of the past haven't died off with the generation from which they spawned. They've simply been passed on to the newer generations. Aside from a loud handful, most white supremacists are covert with their actions, but worse still, more resilient in their beliefs and objectives. The magnanimously rich history of my ancestors has nearly been buried to never be found again, while the pursuit to cripple and oppress my people grows stronger.

Broken families on welfare are essentially properties of the state. To some, state assistance seems more appealing than the notion of effective coparenting. Affordable housing, food stamps, and a myriad of other programs are available, but what perks does the state provide for parents who keep their family unit together? Why would a single mother choose to coparent effectively yet struggle when she can remain a single parent while prospering from state assistance? By no means do I want to see those in need stay in need, but we have to look beyond what someone can receive from the system and look deeper into the ripple effects that permeate in its wake. State assistance provides a means for many, but when it comes to the long-term effects, it's the perfect device to keep impoverished families complacent.

To bring about change within the community, all it really takes is for someone to pass on that valuable information on how to succeed, which in turn will end up trickling down to the next generation. But somehow, the empowering secrets to gaining or keeping wealth never trickle down to under privileged families, which is very ironic, because we live in such a consumer-driven society. Consume, consume, consume. It seems we'll consume material goods gluttonously, but don't consume knowledge in the same way. In 2016, they say that holiday spending in the US exceeded $1 trillion dollars! Yes, you read that right—$1 *trillion*! Consume, consume, consume. On average, 350 million American citizens spent around $500 apiece—and just for the holiday season. I wonder how many of those parents have life insurance, though? As parents, we of course all want to give our kids everything their hearts desire. But you'd think most of those parents who reside in the urban jungles, where violence is king and life expectancy is merely a quarter of a century, would make the ridiculously sound investment of getting life insurance. But you'd be surprised by just how many haven't. See, in the past it was easy to blame society for hiding the keys to financial freedom from black people. Nowadays, technology has totally stifled that notion. Information is the true power, and we live in the era of information itself. It's available to all, and it's free of costs. With the proper research, you can find an affordable life insurance policy that'll give your child a financial cushion in the event of your demise, instead of leaving them with debt. In my opinion, as a parent, having a life insurance policy is a requirement. The fact that some would rather spend fifty dollars per month on lottery tickets is a damn shame.

With all of that said, there's a hidden twist in the fine print of state assistance. Those who receive Supplemental Security Income (SSI) are restricted to the type and amount of life insurance they can receive. If an individual's life insurance is more than what's allowed, his or her benefits stop, along with his or her medical coverage. Does anyone else find this contradictory? So an individual can receive assistance from the state, but when it comes to securing his or her family's financial future in the event of their demise, that individual is restricted and limited in doing so? Thus, it's by design that millions of parents will leave their children with nothing but a tombstone after their passing.

There are millions of lower-income families in that predicament, but what about those parents who make up the middle class? What's their excuse? Nothing is more fulfilling than knowing your children will be okay in your absence. How many of you reading this wish your parents or grandparents had passed down an inheritance to you when they passed? If you weren't privileged enough to experience that, then be the individual to put those wheels in motion for your own kids. And no, it doesn't matter how much money you make. Again, we live in the era of information, and there are a plethora of options you can find when it comes to this issue. You just have to do the research, which is only a click away with Google.

Cue social media. With the tap of a screen, everyone has access to everything. Internet search engines have tainted the days of children sitting with their parents to learn about certain issues in society. We're literally inundated with "content" 24/7/365. And now, being "liked" has replaced being loved. Adults and children alike engage in social media, giving the illusion that we're equals. But we aren't equals in that regard. See, when I was a teenager, there was a distinct difference between the activities my mom and I engaged in. My generation didn't have platforms that allowed us to become someone else in a virtual world. We had to be ourselves and allow our stations in life to form naturally.

This new era of narcissism has spawned a new genre of entertainment—reality TV. Some would argue that certain reality shows are nothing more than a regurgitation of blaxploitation, or even the advent of "whiteploitation". The term *ratchetness* has become an actual way of life for many fatherless teenagers and young adults. Unfortunately, the profits have driven the entertainment industry to label these shows as actual entertainment when in reality they're only tools to control perception. We're blinding ourselves to the latent impacts that further erase the line between a parent and a child. The entertainment industry's job is to push the envelope with messaging, but our jobs, as parents, is to filter through the content our children consume. Will you have to give up some of your guilty pleasures? Yes. But that's what we signed up for the minute we became parents. My mother knew the comedic legend Richard Pryor would say things I was then too young to hear or understand, but that didn't stop her from enjoying his comedy. She simply made sure we didn't enjoy it together. Those are the scenarios in which a parent earns respect. Today's parents are talking, dressing, and sometimes even acting like their teenage children. In general, it's not wise to try to fit in, right? It's all about being yourself and not worrying about the judgment of others. So it's beyond foolish for any parent to try to fit in with his or her children just to earn cool points.

Back in the day, when it came to hip-hop, my mom commented on certain songs that were overtly crass. I'd laugh it off, but it was no longer a laughing matter once I had children of my own. Of course I still enjoy hip-hop, but listening to the words *nigga*, *bitch*, and *hoe* around my kids doesn't feel right within my spirit. It's absurd actually. No father in his right mind wants his daughter to be passive or accept being called a "bitch" or "hoe." But some people hum along to those misogynistic tunes with their kids in the back seat. Why? Is it an attempt to connect with their kids and show they possess that young spirit too? Without standing firm on the line between parent and child, they're subliminally cosigning that song's message, leaving the rest up to their children to decipher on their own.

Interestingly enough, my kids aren't as heavily influenced by hip-hop music as I was growing up. They have a vast taste when it comes to music in general. It's crazy that I've had to shield them from certain types of music. When I was a kid, my mom could put on the radio or play any record from her record collection, and we could sing the songs together. She didn't have to concern herself with censorship in that regard. The music from my mom's generation promoted togetherness, unconditional love, and romance. Those were the days when an entire family could enjoy a Stevie Wonder record and dance together at a backyard barbecue.

Now, when I'm in the car with my kids listening to satellite radio or whatever station, every other word is a curse word. Every other phrase is foul, and every other message is continuing the cycle of negativity in the community. Our children are getting these messages from both sides of the spectrum, from our generation's music as well as their own. There used to be a thing called grown folks' music, which the adults would listen to while playing spades or whatever. The kids would stay off in their own place but still within an earshot, and it was never a problem, because the music, despite being for adults, was still suitable for kids. Coming from the golden era of hip-hop, I find it quite sad that I can't listen to the radio with my kids without having to concern myself with hearing "bitch" this or "nigga" that. Musically, my generation was blessed to also have moments of love and togetherness. But how will this new generation be defined musically? Art will always imitate life. When this new generation reaches their forties, what will the soundtrack of their lives tell their kids about them? I think we know the answer to that question. Picture how those backyard barbecues are going to sound ...

It's not just the music. Even some of the teenage-themed television shows and cartoons openly display negative, skewed perceptions of religion and race, and they're heavy influences on the youth. Subliminal messaging has always existed, but nowadays it's like a free-for-all with no restrictions or boundaries. And who's to blame for that? We are. Because as a nation of parents, we don't come together as a collective voice when it comes to what is morally right for our children. Parenthood has no color or creed and should be an extraordinary body for change when needed, but so many people are distracted. Recreation centers and federally funded arts programs are disappearing. That's a major factor in why these kids spend hours upon hours playing video games. And look, I understand that nothing remains the same, but as parents, shouldn't we try to stick to some of the core principles that made our communities a village?

My mom wasn't overly concerned about the changing times with my generation, because she was still firmly in control of what happened under her own roof. It's almost as if today's parents are scared of their own kids. Teachers are scared of the kids they teach. People are scared of the kids who live in their neighborhoods. That fear has given birth to these new generations who're used to being pacified. Establishing order in your home is a necessity, so why are some parents afraid to take that stand? Maybe it's because a lot of these parents are still children themselves. Still, kids need discipline, and a bunch of them need good old-fashioned ass whoopings. Really, a stern look should be convincing enough to establish that line of respect with your kid. If your child doesn't understand your nonverbal communication, then you've got some work to do. I know I just mentioned ass whoopings, but honestly, spanking kids at every turn for every mistake doesn't really work in the long run. If you spank your kid all the time, they'll become numb and desensitized to it. Ultimately, it's every parent's duty to establish with their children the concept of repercussions for bad behavior, before some police officer or judge eventually does.

Technology is accommodating and has many perks, but social media has essentially created real-time diaries for its users that the whole world can see. The catch is there's no deleting any of it. When I was a kid, mistakes and transgressions were stored in our memory banks and became valuable learning tools rather than trending topics. These days, one foolish act captured on social media can turn into a lifetime scar. It's no secret that employers are even hiring or firing based on one's social media footprint. There are numerous stories of political officials, teachers, and so on losing their jobs because of a seemingly simple tweet. In this day and age, I can't excuse any parent for not treating social media's impacts with levity.

What is it about the cyberworld that people sacrifice their integrity just for a fleeting moment of attention? In my estimation, though theory upon theory can be debated, there's really only one answer: vanity. One afternoon as I scrolled through Instagram, I saw a picture of an infant with five unlit cigarettes in her mouth. I can't explain the sheer disgust and anger that ran through my mind. What some people do on social media to get attention is literally repulsive. Any parent doing the same themselves or condoning such behavior from their kids is even worse. How much self-hate must a person be steeped in to put something as toxic as a cigarette in an infant's mouth? That picture received hundreds of comments and shares. And surely, that woman received the attention she was seeking. But how will that infant feel once she grows up and that picture resurfaces? What would you do if you found out your mother or father did that to you, for the world to see, when you were just a defenseless infant? I'm pretty sure you wouldn't find it amusing to say the least.

It's like people have been blinded by their relentless pursuit for the American dream. But what is the American dream exactly? Going from nothing to something? Having a house with a white picket fence? Getting attention at any and all costs? Having the ability to do whatever, wherever, and however with no accountability? If you ask ten people what their version of the American dream is, you'll probably get ten different answers. A person's version of the American dream is greatly dependent upon how he or she was raised. Money over matter, and vanity over substance seems to be the common thread of the day, but the truth is, none of those things have any real value in the grand scheme of life. What type of person would find amusement in making a mockery of his or her own kid or anyone else's? Well, unfortunately, people like that can be found easily on the Internet, and most times, their foolish acts go without punishment. The cyberworld can be an enemy to human progression, and we must view it as such in order to gain the level of awareness and protection needed to counter its negative aspects. We can't live in fear, but we also can't afford to be careless. You wouldn't leave a minor in a room full of candy, because they would eat everything in sight, right? Well, that room full of candy represents the cyberworld, and it now seems like every-damn-body has a mouth full of cavities.

My mother instilled a powerful truth within me, which is that I alone am worthy. As a kid, I didn't put my self-worth into trendy clothes or flashy jewelry. She helped me build my mind to value positive actions over material gains. That's why when I was an adolescent back on the block, selling drugs was never an option for me. Now, does your kid believe that he or she is worthy? Are you willing to face the reflection of your own parenting? Instilling such a lesson isn't easy for any single mother to do with her son, and in most cases, it takes longer for fatherless children to find their own sense of self-worth. Children must value themselves and feel themselves to be valuable and worthy to their parents. That's an extremely vital component when it comes to parenting in general, because all too often, that lack of self-worth can become the difference between life and death.

So my career was progressing, and sometimes I had to be away from my family for elongated periods. My daughters handled those separations pretty well, but my son would show signs of frustration. One day I got a call from Keisha about his behavior. I wanted to tell myself it was just a phase for him, but something in the pit of my stomach knew there was a deeper issue brewing. But leaving the set to tend to a tantrum wasn't a possibility. I called and we spoke, but I could sense that the conversation was simply not enough for him. One call about his behavior turned into a few, and I knew I'd have a handful to deal with once I returned home.

When you're gone for weeks or months at a time, things can seem to spiral overnight with your kids. Upon my return home, I immediately noticed a difference in K'mari and Amir's relationship. They always enjoyed each other's company, but they now required more individual space, which was understandable given their gap in age. As a woman, Keisha gave our girls the attention needed when I was absent, but our son required something more. Something resonated within me when I realized that. Yeah, he was living the life I'd wished I'd had as a kid, but none of that mattered. His only true desire, at that moment in time, was to have his father present.

I hug and kiss my son on his cheek or forehead every day. The macho, male-bravado mind-set that men are stereotyped with in society is very prevalent in the hood. A lot of our young men grow up missing their fathers' love and affection. In turn, they don't know how to resolve issues among themselves without resorting to violence. The explosion of violence in Chicago is a prime example of that. I know there are a multitude of other valid reasons and excuses, but underneath all of them is a familial undercurrent (or lack thereof) that's inextricably linked to the cause of the problem. As fatherlessness continues to increase, the goons and gangsters are getting younger and younger. Some individuals are so young there's literally nowhere to place them outside of youth detention centers and the like. So they roam the streets and become career criminals before even reaching puberty. Of course, there will always be bad apples, so to say, but all thugs are created, not born. We must face the fact that every gangster we see on the streets was first an innocent child and a human being. Many fatherless kids who end up joining gangs do so merely because they're seeking the feeling of acceptance and protection.

The last thing any father should want is for gang life to seem appealing to his kid. It's a miserable failure if one's kid is willing to die for a cause that is factually nothing but an illusion. And I say such a thing with a grounded respect to all the men who are incarcerated or once were but have turned their lives around for the better. Any real man and any true gangster will tell you the same. No man of principles wants his son to follow in his footsteps when those steps have only led that man to his demise. No man of principles wants his daughter to be initiated into a cause in which the only guaranteed end is jail or death.

Yet people sing, rap, and dance to glorify the gangster lifestyle. They admire gangsters even though they know how their stories always end. In my younger days, being a "dope MC" meant you were skillful at the craft of rapping, not in actually having dealt dope. I'm pretty sure some of my favorite rappers from that time may have indulged in street activities too, but at least those things came second to their artistic expression. It would've been extremely stupid for any rapper from my generation to indict themselves through their music or social media. Oh, but not today's rappers. These guys are proudly snitching on themselves time after time. And yeah, some of them are truly about that life. But for the majority of them, it's really all a hoax; it's only about the perception. They just want to look the part, dress the part, and act the part. In reality, for most of these guys, none of what they spew out is from firsthand experience. The characters they play on record are a far cry from their own true characters as people.

It's troubling that a black man's blackness is validated by his image in the hood. Any environment that is designed to limit you only helps to perpetuate your destruction. "But don't forget where you come from!"

Right? You constantly hear that phrase once you've put the hood mentality behind you where it belongs. I fully understand the notion of remembering one's roots, but our true roots don't originate from the hood. We are the descendants of kings and queens. And I'm saying this in the most literal sense, because that's what we actually originate from.

To clarify, when I say "the hood," I'm not referring to a place, no. I'm speaking about a mentality. To be quite frank, the hood mentality is a sickness. Some of these rappers make millions by glorifying the street life, and they take pride in being able to return to their own hoods as they do so. But why is that? Is it because that's where they learned to become men? Is it because the hood is their metaphorical father and thus acceptance from the streets gives them a sense of validation? Is it because they've fallen victim to the inability to find that validity from within?

Just remember this: a trapped mind is a lost soul. There's a credo that's spoken in every prison across the country: "You can lock my body, but you can't trap my mind." The same notion goes for everyone living in hoods across the globe who're just trying to survive and find a better way. The point I'm making is that you must free your mind. Only a free mind can think outside of the box. Only a free mind can imagine and dream outside of the constraints and boundaries society indoctrinates upon you. And a big part of freeing your mind is to shed all the negative conditioning you've been programmed to believe. Shift your mentality toward the positive.

CHAPTER 8

The House That *House* Built

He who is not contented with what he has, would not be contented with what he would like to have.

—Socrates

In 2012, the final season of *House* was approaching, and it was bittersweet for me. I was a thirty-nine-year-old husband and father of three beautiful children. My oldest was old enough to know that Dr. Foreman was just a character I played on television, but my other two children were still younger and more impressionable. I'd wonder what effects the imagery of their father being a doctor (on TV) would have on them. When a father doesn't understand the importance of the imagery he displays to his children, it can be a recipe for bad things to come. Now, I don't know what careers my children will decide on, but if one of them decides to pursue the field of medicine, I believe the imagery of me as a fictional doctor will have been a big influence.

If kids only have an image of their fathers being in prison, then more than likely, those kids will develop less fear of such a thing happening to them. Some boys even take pride in their fathers' criminal pasts and try to pick up where their fathers left off. It's cyclical. The repeating cycle seems next to impossible to ever stop, but the cycle begins, and thus should end, with the father himself. Sure, plenty of kids grow up and take the opposite paths of their incarcerated fathers, but statistically, most of those kids end up on the same destructive paths that led to the imprisonment of their fathers. As well, lots of them don't even get the privilege of a jail cell, because they end up dead in the streets. Our kids are constantly fed negative imagery when it comes to fatherhood in our communities, so it's our duty to counterattack that by being living examples of positive parenting.

Our youth are being reared in communities where the people praise the hustlers and criminals but not those bright young minds that come back from college with degrees in hand. Our youth live in a society where people literally lose themselves in the cyberworld and take on alter egos to traverse through virtual realities. These viral trends have kids recording themselves doing heinous acts, as if real repercussions don't exist. A lot of kids embody a "live fast, die young" mentality, and crime rates across the country are proof of that fact. Yet most of those kids are products of broken homes where no father is present, so having love and compassion for their fellow man is laughable. The streets are their father figure, and survival of the fittest is a way of life. Some young women have twerked their way to having fifteen minutes of fame on social media. Other young women work hard only to save their money for butt injections and things of that nature. So what happens when these viral generations have babies of their own?

The rhythm of the streets is unpredictable, and every hood enables violence to rule its barter system. Hustle or be hustled. Kill or be killed. Those elements and ways of being are completely counterproductive to simply evolving as a human being, as is everyone's right. Fatherless children in those environments end up striving only to make the block proud. But why isn't bragging about your education, skill, or trade considered a way to really make the block proud? Why doesn't having a college degree impress some women more than having a diamond-encrusted watch or chain? Cars, clothes, hoes, and bankrolls, is that really all a brother knows? We have to challenge these materialistic principles of the American consumer culture and ground ourselves in the doctrines of what's truly valuable in this world.

All in all, lots of kids nowadays have a lack of leadership, and many of them express themselves in misguided ways, which stifles their ability to develop. Though we should never judge a book by its cover, we now live in a world where perception can be more powerful than reality in the court of public opinion. As such, people must be accountable for the negative imagery they glorify, instead of hiding behind the label of artistic expression.

Yes, I'm obviously an artist, and my life is built around my artistic expression. But there's a sound reasoning in everything that I do in that regard. Nothing I do is simply for attention or shock value, and that's what I'm getting at here. A good example of my artistic expression is the character I played on *House*. I purposely constructed the character with a sharp edginess, so those who came from similar circumstances as him could relate. Symbolism is most powerful when it's subliminal, and I understood that. So I didn't want the character to be too square. I wanted him to represent a man who'd fought through a variety of adversities to get where he was. And so, the tattoo on Dr. Foreman's left hand was simply my way of saying to some little kid in the hood, "Hey, you can be a doctor too!" It's absolutely possible to speak positive messages into the world without actually uttering a word.

We can never be afraid to evolve. Evolution is a spiritual voyage, and once we shed environmentally programmed ways of thinking, we can open ourselves up to the possibilities of becoming better people. Though my mother is an ordained clergy of the African Methodist Episcopal Church, and a prayerful Christian woman who raised me to love the Lord, I'd consider myself nondenominational in that regard. I've studied the tenets of Christianity, Judaism, and Islam, and I give credence to all three, quite frankly. That said; I know that prayer requires submission. It's perfectly normal to see a woman fall to her knees and cry for God's help in times of need, but some men are so conditioned not to express any vulnerability that they actually fight against the need to pray. Have we allowed society to transform prayer into a symbol of weakness? I mean it's not like we can turn the spiritual realm off and on. We're all in a constant battle to maintain dignity within our minds and peace within our souls. But some men aren't spiritually equipped to fight those battles, let alone teach their sons how to fight them. So by default that false sense of pride is passed on to their sons, and those boys will stumble into manhood blinded in spirit. It's like the power of God isn't being proclaimed aloud anymore, as if having faith itself has become faint.

As a nation of fathers, we have to strengthen ourselves spiritually, mentally, and emotionally in order to truly progress. We must first do that for ourselves, as individuals, before we can impart any wisdom to our children. When people's faith isn't strong enough to withstand the war of the spirit and the flesh, it's easy for them to give up on everything and stand for nothing, including their own flesh and blood. And the hood is designed to drain us emotionally and spiritually. But here's the thing: if you have what it takes to survive all the elements of the hood day in and day out, you also have what it takes to break free of that mental and spiritual bondage. A lot of young men in the hood don't take a chance on faith, and I believe that's directly attributed to having experienced the deep disappointment caused by the absence of their fathers. If the man who is supposed to protect the family willingly disappears, how can his children have faith in a being they can't touch or see? As a father, the realest thing you should never want to happen is for you to have a negative impact on your child's relationship with God.

Proverbs 13:24 (American Standard Version) says, "He that spareth the rod hateth his son, but he that loveth him chasteneth him betimes." This verse has been interpreted many times over, but it certainly doesn't give a license to physically abuse one's children. The message in this passage is about disciplining children with love. The "rod" is more than just an object; it's a symbol that represents order. And it's every father's job to keep order within his home. All too often, men have left the disciplinary measures to the mothers of their children. In most cultures, it's a mother's natural instinct to discipline her son with enough physical force to make her point.

In 2015, that dynamic was on full display during the riots in Baltimore. In the midst of all the chaos and burning buildings, a woman was seen aggressively pulling her son away from the turmoil. She chided him and even smacked him upside his head to get her point across. That moment was a clear display of a mother implementing her God-given authority over her son. Some pundits couldn't relate to that and even disagreed with her actions, but in the black community that woman was championed for taking a harsh stance to protect her son. Still, some media outlets marked her approach as abuse. Other media outlets even went so far as to say she emasculated her own son. Really? Such ignorance is beyond reproach. That woman was protecting her child by forcefully removing him from that madness. Period! I wonder if those pundits would've preferred for that kid to be dealt with by yet another scared, racist cop instead of his own mother. The fact is, what she did came from the depths of love, a love that only a mother can feel toward her son. And she was completely in her rights to do exactly what she did.

Many people were baffled at why the rioters destroyed parts of their own community in Baltimore. What they didn't realize is no one who grows up within a poverty-stricken neighborhood actually wants to live there. They simply have no other option. You can skip the colorful, glossy images of the hood you see in music videos. The reality is these places lack sufficient resources, infrastructure, and, most importantly, the feeling of security. Thus, to most residents, these places are already in disarray or destroyed. Now, I don't agree with protesting in a violent or destructive manner, but I certainly understood that community's frustrations. For one of the first times, this viral generation showed signs of a revolutionary spirit, and it spread throughout the nation. I saw a glimmer of hope, oddly enough, for the next influx of fatherless children during those riots. But of course, what good is any movement without proper leadership and effective organization?

When your home isn't a place of solace, it feels like an unproductive environment. Many people from my generation became strung out on drugs, while others became full-time hustlers with nothing to show for their deeds but criminal records and street cred. Some of their kids have emerged beyond those circumstances, but more than half have fallen by the wayside and become statistics. Our country will continue to suffer as long as the family unit is desecrated. In this day and age, it should be perfectly normal for a kid to be raised either by his or her biological parents or in an effective coparenting or blended family environment.

There are plenty of able fathers who're unfairly being alienated from their kids, and that's a problem. But to those absentee fathers who deflect the issue by griping about the mothers of their kids only wanting money, what do you expect if you aren't doing your fair share? It's counterproductive to only see your kid every two weeks. I'm not taking anything away from those men whose visitation schedules were set like that via the court system. But in the long run, you will not have any lasting, fruitful impact on your kid's life if you're only spending time with your kid every couple of weeks. And the mother of your child isn't going to give you the credit you might think you deserve either. Do you wake up at the crack of dawn every morning to get your kid prepared for school? Do you help your kid with homework? Do you attend extracurricular activities, parent-teacher conferences, and things of that nature?

It's high time a lot of men stop their self-loathing pity parties and truly examine where they rank in their fatherhood. If you have a high rank, I salute you! If you rank low, do something about it. Leave all the excuses in the trash, and thirst for more. Fight to get better! Scratch and claw by any means necessary to be a more active father to your children. Because remember this: we've only got one life to live on this earth. And time waits for no man.

Parental alienation is a mild form of abuse that many people don't even know exists. For those who're new to the term, parental alienation is the process or result of the psychological manipulation of a child into showing unwarranted fear, disrespect, or hostility toward a parent and/ or other family members. People with bitter hearts purposely instill fear, disrespect, or hostility into their kids, which the kids then project onto the other parent. Though some people can feel the emotional ripples of parental alienation, they still don't identify it as an actual form of abuse. Many fathers have had their own children turned against them. At times, to even the score, those men plant negative images into their kids' minds about their moms. That's a very immature approach, and though they say all is fair in love and war, that's not how it works in the real world. It's psychologically dangerous for parents to paint a negative image of the person they chose to create a life with and to force that image onto their own creations. And all just to feel like they've won in that moment? That kind of thing can foster a lifetime of self-doubt for a child.

To the single mothers who exhibit that type of behavior, when your son or daughter looks into the mirror, do you want the repulsive picture you painted of his or her father staring back? If the answer is yes, you should feel ashamed of yourself. You're planting seeds in your kid that will only bring forth a ruthless and destructive harvest. If the answer is no, then I applaud you and the work you've done on yourself to prevent your emotions from poisoning the mind of your child.

To all those fathers who've fallen off, you don't have the luxury of catching amnesia just because your relationship with the mother of your child didn't work. That woman is the mother of your child, period. Why would you even try to turn her kid against her? Plus, when it's all said and done, neither of you wins, and only your child will lose.

People dehumanize one another, and it's alarming to know that it's happening right now as you're reading this book. Right now, a kid somewhere is literally being trained to hate a person he or she should love unconditionally. These situations can create extremely daunting mental effects, as kids' ingrained concepts of love will surely carry with them throughout their adulthood. For the most part, parents raise their kids based on their own upbringings. Maybe they witnessed their own parents perpetuating negative images of one another, and so, in a cyclical pattern, they then rehash the same behavior and spew hatred toward their children's other parent. Subsequently, those children are held captive in a mental hell of sorts, causing many to lash out violently in retribution. Thus, the hatred some parents perpetuate often backfires on them. How important is it for you to win a war of words? To exhibit such a wicked form of verbal combat, with your child in the cross fire, is a clear reflection of your character. Just because you feed, clothe, and nurture your child doesn't give you justification to manipulate your child's underdeveloped mind to go against his or her other parent.

You should instill positive images of your kid's other parent just for the sake of your child having a solid inner identity for himself or herself. And yeah, when you consider the financial components, visitation rights, and so on, coparenting effectively can be complicated. But if you always keep your kid as the focal point, you really can't go wrong. To a lot of men, that financial part can be very frustrating. Some women wield a father's financial obligations as a weapon of mass destruction, but those women need to know that, in the long run, the only destruction they're causing is to their own children's paternal relationships. So change that approach for the betterment of your kid.

Don't let the streets become a source of comfort and belonging for your kid. When you come from where a lot of us come from, seeing crack vials wedged in between slabs of concrete is normal. But you can teach your kids not to use their circumstances as a crutch but rather as fuel to ascend productively. In the midst of all adversities, always make sure your home is a safe place of refuge for your children.

When it comes to fatherhood, there are never-ending questions, which come with layer upon layer of answers, but the simplest fix within our power is changing the narrative on the issue. As men, let's shift our perspective. If an inmate has the mental capacity to turn a prison cell into a space of relative peace, anyone who's not locked up has an unlimited capability to change his or her circumstances. In many cases, once men are incarcerated, they attempt to be the best fathers they can be from behind those bars. But it's really sad that it took these men being locked up for them to all of a sudden see the importance of their fatherhood. We all have the power of choice, but wisdom is earned individually. And unfortunately, too many men are becoming wise men from within those cold, dank cells. If a kid can only learn what not to be from his or her father, then that man didn't really live for his kid. There's no reprieve in such lessons.

CHAPTER 9
A Warrior's Kingdom

A smirk was all on my face,
like damn, that man's face is just like my face.
So pop, I forgive you for all the shit that I lived through.
It wasn't all your fault, homie, you got caught.
—Jay-Z, "Moment of Clarity"

I've earned my place atop the throne of my bloodline. As the oldest, and only male grandson, being the overseer of our family legacy is such an esteemed and prestigious position. And yet forgiving a parent who once abandoned you is one of the most difficult things to try to conquer within yourself. All the pains and anguishes attached to growing up fatherless have no expiration date. Even though I've broken the cycle, a new set of equations has emerged. What could my father possibly share with my children? Am I now robbing them of an experience with their biological grandfather? Is it selfish of me to not try to foster a relationship between my father and his biological grandchildren?

I rarely speak about my father, so my kids rarely ask about him. But as they've gotten older, they've inquired about him and the nature of our relationship. Honestly, all I can give them is exactly what I'm giving you right now. No matter what inner obstacles I may overcome, no matter how much forgiveness I can find in my heart, to have a working, functioning relationship with any person, it takes two to tango. And when it comes to my father, it has been a constant one-way street in that regard.

When I was a child, maybe my bitterness ran deeper than I was willing to admit. Maybe that's true for most fatherless kids. But by not forgiving my father, I was actually doing more harm to myself by continuing to carry that burden alone.

The ultimate level of compassion is forgiveness, and pride is forgiveness's archenemy. If someone kept a scorecard of how many battles pride versus forgiveness has won on this earth, I'm pretty sure pride would be a close second. But pride in of itself is a selfish thing, and fatherlessness can rob you of the empathy needed to choose forgiveness. An unforgiving heart eventually ends up killing off its host, though, if you're reading this book and you haven't forgiven your father for abandoning you as a child, you have to find it in yourself to finally release all that pain and anguish. Free yourself from that emotional bondage! No, it's not an easy thing to accomplish, but it's absolutely necessary in order for you to truly reach your higher self. Renew your mind and your heart! Not only do you owe it to yourself, but you deserve it.

So in one breath, I'm a grown man who's made a good life for himself and his family. And yet in another, I'm still a fatherless child searching for answers. What we accomplish in the secular realm means nothing in the eyes of the Most High. How we are, in a spiritual sense, determines how we will ultimately be judged. Many single parents carry bitterness in their hearts, and they develop selfish attitudes that corrupt their souls and thus endanger the souls of their own children as well. My mother is a forgiving woman, but how I chose to deal with my father's absence was out of her control. The lane was always open for us to have a conversation about him, but my life's journey propelled me to a place where neither he nor that conversation was needed. I guess you could say my success was the perfect decoy.

That's a game we all play. We think success will fill the voids that can't be measured by currency. We're afraid to show our vulnerabilities, and we hide behind our possessions and our pride. In my 30's, maybe I was still too immature to admit I needed closure for myself when it came to my father. One glance at the life I'd built was enough to sweep those emotions under the rug. The nonexistent relationship with my father hadn't stopped me from paying the bills, spending time with my children, or loving my wife. So what could reconciliation with him really offer me? Many single parents find themselves trying to answer the same question in relation to their kids. To those single parents who've tried relentlessly to get the absent parent to participate in their children's lives, I empathize with your frustration. But again, when you put your child first, giving up can't be an option.

When Jesus was led to Golgotha to be crucified, some of the spectators he'd once shepherded then chanted for his death. At any point, he could've broken from those shackles and saved himself. But Jesus knew his purpose was much greater than self-indulgence. *To whom much is given, much is expected.* That statement doesn't pertain to a chosen few; it's meant for everyone. Being a parent is a supreme responsibility, so take it as such. Imagine being held close in the arms of God. That's similar to the feeling a kid gets when embraced by his or her father. Too many men have forfeited those roles and have squandered the endless blessings of fatherhood. Regardless of how much money you're worth, your kid really doesn't care. Every kid desires the same exact thing when it comes to his or her father, and that's the feeling of being loved and protected. Depriving children of those feelings is tragic.

So, as a man, what type of kingdom are you building? Is it built on how many zeros are in your bank account? If so, your foundation will eventually crack and crumble. Most who are well off and in tune with the true values of life will tell you that money doesn't equate to happiness. So many people base their happiness on material gains versus finding happiness in each and every moment of their lives. But what good are your accomplishments and possessions if you have a stingy heart? They say the true measure of a man is his character, and that is real. You can have all the money in the world, but at the end of the day, if you're an absent, inactive father? Your real worth is absolutely nothing.

And that reality can break a weak-minded man who has let his fatherhood fall to the wayside. Beyond the ethereal feeling of love, a person must also be fueled by the repetition of discipline when it comes to their kids. Parenthood is a lot like boxing, in that you have to be able to make the necessary adjustments on the fly when needed. We all were kids once, so we're all innately aware that kids go through phases as they grow. Even as they become adults, it's just another more weighted set of phases. I'm saying that to say, parenthood is synonymous to that, as it too happens in phases. So, if you're a man that's let your fatherhood run astray, recalibrate and adapt. You still have a chance to right your wrongs. Don't become a prisoner of your guilt, and find comfort in sulking within your failures. Accept what you've done, embrace the domino effects it's had on your kids, and their mother, and then walk fearlessly through the flames of change. Better yourself.

Realize that whatever your situation may be, there's someone praying for the things you take for granted, e.g., some people can't even have children naturally. And here you are forsaking yours. Even more tragic, some people have buried their children. And that's literally something that brings tears to my eyes, because no parent ever wants to face such a terrible circumstance. But it happens, every single day at that. And here you are going about your days as if you don't have kids wandering around on the planet. Atone for your actions. Realize the aftermath will be whatever it is, not some idyllic picture you have in your head, but the key is you have to accept it. And you have to also know that in the marathon of life, it'll pay off in some way, for you and your kids.

No excuses, actions over words. And if you can't free yourself from that mental and emotional bondage which was self-inflicted to begin with, then that's a really sad thing. You'll have to walk with that weight on your conscience until you take your last breath in the flesh. The kicker is, that weight will still be with you in spirit even in the hereafter. That's the real truth, no matter what your beliefs may be. And that's simply because energy is real, even the science community will attest to that. And spiritual energy is eternal. Now, let that marinate and digest it. Our bodies, our flesh are mortal, they have expiration dates. But our spirits never die they simply evolve into different planes of existence. Thus, one's fatherhood, motherhood, brotherhood, and sisterhood never cease to exist.

They're everlasting bonds that can be felt in the world of the seen, and in the world of the unseen. Think about that. Then think about the balance in your karmic bank account. Are you in debt, or do you have a surplus?

Cats steady want to talk about what's real, well let's talk about it then. Parenthood is real. Fatherhood is real. And if you're not holding up your end of the bargain, the consequences that come along with that are very much real too. You see, when you're ignorant and make the wrong move, that's just a lesson guising itself as a mistake. But when you know better, and you make the same mistake twice, that's an indication of your character, and what you stand for. Now, no one is perfect, but most of us know better. And every path to victory is arduous.

Cats are out here steady talking about they're cut from the cloth of greatness, but a lot of their actions subtract from such a notion. You can have all the money, and success, but if you're not taking care of your kids in an active manner, in my eyes, you're a straight sucker. Any man whose not holding it down for his kids is lame. And that's the new narrative on this issue. That's the new paradigm shift in the culture when it comes to fatherhood. Every man who isn't taking care of his own seeds isn't a king at all beloved. Those dudes will now be classified, and identified as clowns, suckers, and lames. And we'll give you a window of time to repair your situation, but once that window closes, you'll forever be branded with those labels. And we don't care who you are, or what you do, from now on we're no longer accepting that kind of behavior from the men in our communities.

Sister, sister, we see you too. And we demand more from you as well. The catch phrase now amongst women is, *boss up*, right? And we're all for that, but it's no longer acceptable to shame yourself just to make a dollar. Please believe, I'm not on some "mister goody two shoes" stuff either, I'm just speaking truth. That time has come and gone, and now a new line is being drawn in the sand.

We're no longer normalizing all of that over sexualized behavior from our women, nor will we glorify it. It's unacceptable. That is not how we want our sons and daughters to perceive their own mothers. The femininity in every woman is powerful in of itself, as the universe intended. You are the bearers of life! None would even be here if it weren't for women. I fully support women's empowerment, pay equality in the workplace, and things of that nature. And I'm certainly not passing judgment, but when will we as a society evolve beyond the notion that sex sells?

It's overbearing at this point. From fashion ads, to car commercials, to fast food ads, why is it always sex, sex, sex? And there's a huge difference between what's raunchy or gratuitous, and what's organically sexy. There's a world of difference between *sensuality*, and *sexuality*. Sensuality is a natural state where art can take flight through expression. Sexuality is carnal, and thus can be influenced by lower vibrational frequencies like vanity, ego, and lust.

So, over-indulgent sexuality combined with social media equals degraded integrity, thoughtless desperation, and meaningless gratification. And to think, there are thousands upon thousands of women, who are mothers, subjecting themselves to such circumstances on a daily basis. Nah, us men of principles aren't with that. We want more from you sister, because we know that kind of unsavory behavior is beneath you. We know that you too have greatness within you. And some of you may feel as though you've had no other choice, or you gotta' do what you gotta' do, but as the laws of the universe would have it; no one can believe in you more than you believe in yourself. You'll never recognize the pedestal of any man's respect if you don't respect yourself. And you'll never feel the comfort of any man's love if you don't first love yourself.

CHAPTER 10

OG Status

The weak can never forgive. Forgiveness is the attribute of the strong.

—Mahatma Gandhi

A re you ready to forgive? It's an incredibly empowering feeling. An unforgiving heart wallows in misery and loathing, ultimately hurting the person carrying its weight infinitely more than whomever they choose not to forgive. Plus, not forgiving stifles your ability to evolve and ascend. The chance to evolve won't ever force itself upon you, but life will present you with plenty of opportunities to do so. One of our key purposes in this life is to master oneself, and two huge components of self-mastery are acceptance and empathy. Being able to gain understanding is relative to many moving parts, in my opinion. Yet the ability to find acceptance and have empathy are fully within our grasps at all times, in any situation. More times than not, we must enforce these capabilities on situations that derive from our pasts. When someone hurts or disappoints us, we all mentally rationalize and justify our reactions. Then we conjure up the ways in which we believe that person should regain our trust. If those things don't happen in the ways that we prefer, we place those people back on emotional treadmills to chase our forgiveness.

I'd always wanted my father to rectify our relationship in a specific way. When he failed to deliver to those standards in my mind, it was easy for me to fall back into my comfort zone in regard to him. But see, when you grow spiritually, your old mind becomes akin to your enemy. That old mind stays in a continuous cycle of pain and disappointment, which are fueled by an underlying selfishness. My father hadn't yet renewed his mind when it came to me. Though, in my late 30's, mine was renewed in many ways when it came to him, maybe it wasn't as renewed as I'd like to believe. Sure, I'd cracked the door open for us to converse, but every time we spoke, it was as if he was looking at all his past failures dead in the face. He couldn't seem to withstand that weight. I guess one could say that I am the living and breathing representation of his greatest failure in life. And for me, he's the living and breathing representation of one of my biggest internal obstacles. Regardless, I am still his son, and biologically he's my father. Thus, it's his sole responsibility to escape his old mind and finally face his fears when it comes to me.

Many parents allow their old minds to steer and control their relationships. There's so much hurt festering within them that they tear one another down, verbally and otherwise, as if they haven't built lifelong bonds together. Their old minds are more than capable of keeping them at odds because they feed off of emotional immaturity and ego. Renewing your mind is the first step to finding real peace, not only within yourself, but also within relationships that were once caustic. But first, you have to acknowledge that your old mind actually exists. Second, you need to understand that one of your primary purposes in life is to master self. The greatest trick the old mind has is that it advertises itself as your biggest cheerleader. It'll root for you when you feel as though no one else cares. It'll pick you up in moments when no one else will. That's how you become conditioned to trust it. The old mind can easily camouflage itself into every aspect of your life, unbeknownst to you, and it only gets stronger each time you look into the mirror without realizing it's controlling you.

I guess in a barbaric sense, it's natural to want the person who's hurt you to feel your pain. And the last thing the old mind wants you to do is be forgiving toward someone who has hurt you, simply because in that very moment of forgiveness, the old mind receives a thousand deathblows. It whimpers to you, saying things like "After all the tears we've shed, all the pain and sorrow we've been through, how dare you forgive the father of your child for not stepping up to the plate?" or "How dare you forgive your child's mother for what she's done to us?" But see, your old mind doesn't really love you or your children. It never has. The only thing it has ever truly cared about is your pain, because it knows that when you're in pain, you're completely blinded to its true actions. I too was blinded by the pain my father caused me, mentally and emotionally. Quite honestly, I was motivated by it and, even further, found a comfort in it. That attitude was nothing but toxicity for my spirit. Forgiveness is one of the hardest things to accomplish for this reason; it's the ultimate catalyst to freedom. And forgiveness begins with the renewal of your mind. Once I realized that, I had to fully surrender to the renewal of my mind when it came to matters of my father.

In order to truly understand the constant battle between good and evil, you have to know where that battle actually takes place. Even though the brain has its physical function within the body, our minds are invisible to us. That can be dangerous when it comes to the old mind because your old mind will never give you access to the power of forgiveness. It simply goes on controlling you in secret. It keeps you from adapting and restructuring the relationship you have with your kid's other parent for the better. Every time you feel a desire to reconcile, your old mind rehashes all the past pains associated with that person and plays them over and over again in your mind. See, your old mind doesn't need any new tricks. It has enough of your past disappointments stored on its hard drive to control and dictate your emotions at any given moment. The old mind is where all the negative lives. That's why the road to forgiveness is such an uphill battle. A weak mind would suffocate itself trying to be forgiving because forgiveness is an act of real strength, godly strength! Only the strong can truly forgive—please know that! There's an immense power shift that happens in the renewing of one's mind toward the positive, and it's imperative that you realize forgiveness is a tremendous, life-changing action.

A renewed mind is where your peace resides. Even though America is a nation filled with the wanting of recognition and adulation, forgiveness doesn't require an audience, cheerleaders, or even attention. Authentic forgiveness is merely an agreement made with oneself, in one's own heart and mind, to release oneself from the bondage of expectations. Everyone wants to feel as if they're in control of everything, but that's just not the way reality actually works. The old mind will tell one scorned parent that forgiving the other means giving up control to that other parent. See how that works? As strange as it seems, it's actually pretty simple to decipher too. Such a thing often happens when a man who's failed to handle his responsibilities of fatherhood tries to change course. In such situations, the old mind will whisper to that single mom, "After all you alone have done, you'd better not let him just pop back up into your kid's life!" See how pride and ego have such a harmonious relationship? They know exactly how to manipulate our thoughts to accomplish their self-ish goals, and they never ever miss an opportunity to do so. Thus, if you have an unforgiving heart, you're a prime target to be enslaved within the purgatory of your past.

Leaders from previous generations used the power of forgiveness to help shape and forever change our cultural landscape. MLK's entire movement was built on the power of forgiveness, and look what transpired thereafter. As parents, we have to channel that very same strength to save the family structure in this country. And that should be a much easier thing to overcome than segregation, Jim Crow, and the like. If the Freedom Riders from the civil rights era could literally look evil in the face and say "I forgive you," then we should be able to employ the same courageousness when it comes to saving our families in this nation. The wars we allow to ensue among our loved ones can be dissolved with the simple renewing of our minds. As they say, family is forever. So why enable menial disagreements to fester until they become irreconcilable differences? Much too often, people let issues linger and grow, like fungus or mold, until their lives are nothing but a collection of memories blowing in the wind. In the end, as I can tell you from experience itself, it's just not worth it. Life is way too precious.

Lest we forget just how delicate and fragile life itself really is, to you single mothers, if your kid's father were to die today, how would you feel?

Would you feel guilt? Remorse? Dare I say, even a tad of shame? If your answer is yes, then you, my dear, are taking this blessed thing called life for granted. And to you absent fathers, if you were to die today, what would your child say about you, huh? Would you have left a positive impact on your kid's life, or would you be nothing more than a picture on a cheap T-shirt with the letters *RIP* above your face? Forgiveness has the ability to change how we approach everything. Some believe that in order to forgive, you have to engage in some sort of conversation with the other person. Though that can be soothing, that's not necessarily required. As I stated earlier, authentic forgiveness is actually a solitary thing. All else is relative to whatever the circumstances may be, but there really is no need to be afraid.

The inability to forgive is one of the paramount reasons why father-lessness is such an epidemic. If God, or whomever you believe in, can offer forgiveness, then we can't allow our mortal minds to destroy the blessings of the infinite. When you grow up fatherless, it can be difficult to learn how to forgive people in general. And when the pattern of fatherlessness is repeated, those men are unwittingly imposing their embattled pasts onto their own children. As with me, even when that cycle is broken, remnants of fatherlessness can still infiltrate your relationship with your children. And that's scary. And yet so many parents knowingly allow their children to witness their unforgiving hearts toward the other parent. It's every parent's job to sacrifice certain things for the sake of their children, and that also includes the disdain they may have for the other parent.

I stepped into a new level of maturity once I embraced the fact that my father wasn't my enemy. He was simply a man, just like I am. As human beings, we're all flawed in our own ways. So whenever he and I spoke from that point on, I no longer carried any anger or resentment in my heart. I simply stood in empathy and compassion. I even tried to envision his perspective. Of course, I still didn't agree with his decisions in the past when it came to me, but I'd finally freed myself from all the pain and disappointment connected to those decisions. By truly forgiving my father, I finally found a peace with our connection in this life. I'd shed that "I'm here, ain't I?" mind-set and fathered my own children from a renewed ṁind. It's not my presence that's a present to my kids; it's my essence that ṁs. My perspective broadened for the better. I'd single-handedly raised the bar and set a new standard of fatherhood for the men in my bloodline. And that's what it's all about, isn't it? Victory! Without having truly forgiven my father, I never would've reached this level of consciousness. If you grew up in a fatherless environment, the bar of fatherhood has been set extremely low for you. But once you yourself become a father, exhibit forgiveness for the failures of your own father so that you too can change the course of your family's history.

Recently, my sister called to inform me that our biological father had passed on ... I felt no angst or regret. I felt no discontent or heartache. What I felt was a compassionate sadness for him. What I felt was a sense of peace for him. His life's journey was uniquely his, and he lived it the way he saw fit. I pray he's now at peace with himself, and he's now at peace with me, along with his other children. May God rest his soul.

I'd also be remiss if I didn't mention, upon the writing of this book, Aiyanna's mother died after an arduous battle with cancer. Her passing has affected our daughter in the most obvious of ways, and it has been challenging for our family to say the least. This lasting event has put my fatherhood to the test in ways that I could've never anticipated. Yet, we endure, we persevere, and we do so as one. May God rest her soul.

In closing, if there's one takeaway from this book that I want you to hold on to, it's the infinite power of choice. We always have the power of choice at our disposal. Please remember that! We are living in a time when fatherhood itself is an extremely crucial component to the advancement of our communities at large and to the preservation of those sacred family bonds that have helped to propel us to this point. So this is a call to action! It's time to activate fatherhood throughout our communities and the world abroad. Of course, each and every man has his own story, and this one is simply mine. But no matter what any man's story is, when it comes to fatherhood, he always has an undefeatable weapon in the power of choice. There really are no excuses.

To all my fellow fathers out there who're actively parenting their children, I salute you. I respect you. I stand in arms alongside you. To all those men out there who have yet to become fathers, please take heed of everything I've laid out in these pages. Make the right choices. And to those men who've failed in their fatherhood and those who're teetering on the brink of failure, I hope my story has inspired you to grab the bull by the horns and do better. As long as you have breath in your lungs, you can change the course of your fatherhood. So fight for it! Find your strength and courage in knowing that you're doing so for your child. And to all the single mothers out there, no matter your story, we salute you. We respect you. We admire you. And to all the women out there whose kids' fathers are actively in their kids' lives? Cherish that, nurture that, and give thanks!

Let us celebrate fatherhood! Let us activate fatherhood! Let us be proud of our fatherhood!

With peace and love,
Omar Epps